JESUS AS THE SON OF MAN IN MARK

Andrés A. Tejada-Lalinde

2019

Apart from revisions that were made since 2014, this book constitutes the thesis submitted in partial fulfillment of the requirements for the degree of
MASTER OF ARTS
in
RELIGIOUS STUDIES
at
Florida International University
in
2014

ACKNOWLEDGMENTS

First and foremost, I thank God, who through the Holy Spirit continually guides me and from whom I inferred through Christ's Spirit that the Bible is a book of unique and utmost importance. To God I give credit all that is good and true in this thesis.

I would like to thank my family, especially my parents, for their continued love and support throughout the whole process.

I would like to thank my Major Professor, Dr. Erik Larson, Chair and Associate Professor at FIU, for his continual help throughout the whole process. I thank him for the advice he lent me, using his extensive knowledge of the topic and for helping me with the languages of Hebrew, Aramaic, and Greek. I thank him also for all the suggestions of reference, for his feedback on the thesis, and for his advice in general.

I would like to thank committee member Dr. Christine Gudorf, former Professor at FIU, for her suggestions of reference, her feedback on the thesis, and for her prompt responses to my inquiries.

I would also like to thank committee member Dr. Ana María Bidegain, Professor at FIU, for her general helpfulness and likewise for her prompt responses to my inquiries, especially given that I usually submitted forms at the last minute.

I would also like to thank Dr. Oren B. Stier, former Graduate Program Director and currently Professor at FIU, for his advice and for making himself available on the occasions when I had any questions.

I would like to thank Dr. Derek Allen, Lead Pastor of Christ Centered Church, for his feedback on the thesis and for his advice as well.

I would also like to thank Joey Wood, former House Church Pastor of Christ Centered Church and currently Associate Pastor at Crawford Baptist Church, for his advice and support.

Copyright Year: 2019.

Copyright Notice: by Andrés A. Tejada-Lalinde. All rights reserved.

The above information forms this copyright notice: © *2019 by Andrés A. Tejada-Lalinde. All rights reserved.*

ISBN: 978-0-578-22008-6

Bowman Jr., Robert M. and J. Ed Komoszewski. Putting Jesus in His Place: The Case for the Deity of Christ. Grand Rapids, Michigan: Kregel Publications, 2007. Kindle edition. Copyright © 2007. Quotations taken from locations 643, 647, and 2,766 of 4,522 (44 words) used by permission of the publisher. All rights reserved.

Boyarin, Daniel. *The Jewish Gospels: The Story of the Jewish Christ*. New York: The New Press, 2012 (the paperback edition I used was published in 2013). Quotations taken from pages 26, 67, and 68 (83 words) reproduced by permission of the publisher. Excerpt from *The Jewish Gospels: The Story of the Jewish Christ*— Copyright © 2012 by Daniel Boyarin. Reprinted by permission of The New Press. www.thenewpress.com

Burkett, Delbert. *The Son of Man Debate: A History and Evaluation*. Cambridge, UK: Cambridge University Press, 1999. © Cambridge University Press 1999. Quotations taken from pages 5, 8, 13, 69, and 84 (52 words) reproduced with permission of the Licensor through PLSclear.

Casey, Maurice. *The Solution to the 'Son of Man' Problem*. New York: T & T Clark International, 2007. Kindle edition. Copyright © 2007. Quotations taken from locations 1,002; 1,043; 1,045; 3,159; and 4,378 of 6,420 (59 words) reproduced by permission of T & T Clark, an imprint of Bloomsbury Publishing Plc.

Charles, R.H., trans. *The Book of Enoch the Prophet*. Introduction by R. A. Gilbert. New Introduction by Lon Milo DuQuette. California/ Massachusetts: Weiser Books, 2012 ed. Kindle edition. Material excerpted from *The Book of Enoch the Prophet* by R.H.

Charles used with permission from Red Wheel Weiser, LLC Newburyport, MA, www.redwheelweiser.com.

Craig, William Lane. *Reasonable Faith: Christian Truth and Apologetics*. 3rd edition. Illinois: Crossway, 2008. Quotations from pages 292, 299, and 327 (103 words) taken from *Reasonable Faith: Christian Truth and Apologetics (3rd Edition)* by William Lane Craig, © 2008. Used by permission of Crossway, a publishing ministry of Good News Publishers, Wheaton, IL 60187, www.crossway.org.

Crossan, John Dominic. *The Historical Jesus: The Life of a Mediterranean Jewish Peasant*. Harper Collins e-books, 2010. Kindle edition. Copyright © 2010. Quotations taken from location 6,026 of 12,350 (4 words) reproduced by permission of HarperCollins Publishers.

Encyclopædia Britannica. "Targum (Biblical Literature)." Last accessed March 26, 2019. http://www.britannica.com/EBchecked/topic/583515/Targum. 39 words from web page reproduced by permission of *Encyclopædia Britannica*.

Evans, Craig A. *Fabricating Jesus: How Modern Scholars Distort the Gospels*. Illinois: Inter Varsity Press, 2006. Kindle edition. Copyright © 2006. Quotations taken from pages 38, 39, 46, 48, 50, and 51 (99 words) used by permission of InterVarsity Press, P.O. Box 1400, Downers Grove, IL 60515, USA. www.ivpress.com

Hurtado, Larry W. and Paul L. Owen et al. *'Who is This Son of Man?': The Latest Scholarship on a Puzzling Expression of the Historical Jesus*. Edited by Larry W. Hurtado and Paul L. Owen. New York: Bloomsbury T & T Clark,

2011. Copyright © 2011. Quotations taken from pages 23, 35, 47, 59, 60, 67, 83, 86, 132-134, 151, and 174 (215 words) reproduced by permission of T & T Clark, an imprint of Bloomsbury Publishing Plc.

Johansson, Daniel. "'Who Can Forgive Sins but God Alone?' Human and Angelic Agents, and Divine Forgiveness in Early Judaism." *Journal for the Study of the New Testament* 33, no. 4 (June 1, 2011): 351-374. ATLA Religion Database with ATLASerials, EBSCOhost (last accessed January 18, 2014). Copyright © 2011. Quotations taken from pages 352 and 353 (10 words) reprinted by Permission of SAGE Publications, Ltd.

Milavec, Aaron. *The Didache: Text, Translation, Analysis, and Commentary.* Translated by Aaron Milavec. Minnesota: Liturgical Press, 2003. Copyright 2003 by Order of Saint Benedict. Published by Liturgical Press, Collegeville, Minnesota. Quotation taken from page 37 (13 words) used with permission.

Moule, C.F.D. *The Origin of Christology.* Cambridge, UK: Cambridge University Press, 1977. © Cambridge University Press 1977. Quotations taken from page 15 (32 words) reproduced with permission of the Licensor through PLSclear.

Müller, Mogens. *The Expression 'Son of Man' and the Development of Christology: A History of Interpretation.* Sheffield, UK: Equinox, 2012 paperback edition; "First published in hardback in 2008." Quotation taken from page 419 (6 words) republished with permission of Taylor & Francis Informa UK Ltd – Books, from, Mogens. *The Expression 'Son of Man' and the Development of Christology: A History of Interpretation*, Mogens Müller, 2012 paperback edition; "First published in hardback in 2008"; permission conveyed through Copyright Clearance Center, Inc., www.copyright.com.

NLT Parallel Study Bible. Senior Editor Comfort, Philip W. Carol Stream, Illinois: Tyndale House Publishers, Inc., 2011. Quotations from pages 1,538; 1,549; 1,554; 1,562; 1,782; 1,847; and 1,960 (136 words) are taken from the *NLT Parallel Study Bible*, copyright © 2011 by Tyndale House Foundation. Notes and Bible helps used by permission of Tyndale House Publishers, Inc., Carol Stream, Illinois 60188. All rights reserved.

Rowe, Robert D. "Is Daniel's 'Son of Man' Messianic?" In *Christ the Lord: Studies in Christology presented to Donald Guthrie*, edited by Harold H. Rowdon. Leicester, UK: Inter-Varsity Press, 1982, 71-96. © Inter-Varsity Press, Leicester, 1982. Quotation taken from page 71 (23 words) reproduced with permission of the Licensor through PLSclear.

The Holy Bible, English Standard Version® (ESV®). Unless otherwise indicated, all Scripture quotations are from the ESV® Bible (The Holy Bible, English Standard Version®), copyright © 2001 by Crossway, a publishing ministry of Good News Publishers. Used by permission. All rights reserved.

The New Oxford American Dictionary. Second Edition. New York: Oxford University Press, Inc e-book, 2010. Kindle edition. Copyright © 2010 by Oxford University Press. Quotation taken from location 975,126 of 1,082,596 (16 words total) reproduced with permission of the Licensor through PLSclear.

ABSTRACT OF THE THESIS
JESUS AS THE SON OF MAN IN MARK
by
Andrés A. Tejada-Lalinde
Florida International University, 2014
Miami, Florida
Professor Erik Larson

Scholars have often seen the interpretation of the Son of Man as crucial in discovering Jesus' self-understanding, given that the expression occurs so frequently and almost exclusively on Jesus' lips. After ascertaining the authenticity of the Son of Man sayings, I carry out the exegesis in the Gospel of Mark using a methodology consisting of examining Biblical passages within the context of the Bible as a whole and of historical-critical and philological perspectives. Also, the narrative context of the sayings is taken into account. I show that the Son of Man is a Messianic title derived from Daniel 7:13, and that the book of Daniel's content and themes were used as a basis for the Son of Man sayings themselves. In addition to using the Son of Man as a Messianic title, Jesus used the title as a claim to divinity.

TABLE OF CONTENTS

ACKNOWLEDGMENTS iii
ABSTRACT OF THE THESIS x
- I. INTRODUCTION 1
  - A. Various Interpretations 1
  - B. Methodology 7
    1. Exegetical Method 7
    2. Outline 10
- II. THE USE OF THE EXPRESSION AROUND JESUS' TIME 12
  - A. The Use of "Son of Man" Around Jesus' Time .. 12
    1. Aramaic: Jesus' Native Language 12
    2. Use of "Son of Man" in the Tanakh 14
    3. Use of "Son of Man" Before and During the Time of Jesus 16
       a. The Extant Occurrences 16
       b. Reconstruction of "the Son of Man" into Aramaic 18
    4. Use of "Son of Man" in Later Jewish Literature 21
  - B. Daniel and Apocalyptic Literature 26
    1. Daniel: The Apocalyptic Book of the Bible .. 26
    2. The Qumran Literature 32
    3. The Similitudes of Enoch 34
    4. 4 Ezra 37
    5. Rabbinic Literature 39
    6. Son of Man Concept? 40
  - C. "The Son of Man" in the New Testament: The Question of Authenticity 41
    1. Double-Dissimilarity 43
    2. Multiple Attestation 50
    3. Coherence 51

		4. Criterion of Embarrassment 52
	D.	Jesus Was Referring Exclusively to the "Son of Man" from Daniel 7:13..53
III.		EXEGESIS OF MARK...56
	A.	The Son of Man Sayings in Mark...........................56
	B.	The Son of Man as a Messianic Title....................86
		1. Jesus Used the Son of Man as a Messianic Title 86
		2. Jesus' Use of a Messianic Title That Was Unknown and Ambiguous 93
		3. The Early Church's Use of the Title and of the Book of Daniel...97
IV.		THE SON OF MAN AS DIVINE MESSIAH 107
	A.	The Divine Messiah 107
		1. The Heavenly "Son of Man" from Daniel. 107
		2. The Son of Man: A Claim to Divinity 112
	B.	Conclusion... 119
		1. Summary 119
		2. Implications 121
BIBLIOGRAPHY... 123		

I. INTRODUCTION
A. Various Interpretations

Over the past two millennia, scholars have been endeavoring to ascertain what was meant by the expression "the Son of Man," which was so frequently and almost exclusively used by the peripatetic thaumaturge from Nazareth known as Jesus.[1] The expression occurs 81 times in the Gospels, 77 of which come from Jesus (with two additional ones in indirect speech).[2] Yet outside of the Gospels, it occurs only on one further occasion (with the definite article) in the New Testament. Despite being used so often by Jesus, an explicit explanation is never given in the Gospels (or in any book of the New Testament) as to what Jesus meant by the designation of "the Son of Man."[3] Jesus is never even called "the Son of Man" by Paul or any of the Twelve.[4] It seems that Christians had no fixed interpretation

---

[1] Delbert Burkett, *The Son of Man Debate: A History and Evaluation*, (Cambridge, UK: Cambridge University Press, 1999), 2; Metzger Müller et al., *The Oxford Companion to the Bible* (New York: Oxford University Press, 1993), 711.

[2] *Accordance Bible Software* (version 10). Statistics were gathered using the English Standard Version (ESV). In John 5:27, "Son of Man" has no definite article in the underlying Greek (Benjamin E. Reynolds, "The Use of the Son of Man Idiom in the Gospel of John," in *'Who is This Son of Man?': The Latest Scholarship on a Puzzling Expression of the Historical Jesus*, ed. Larry W. Hurtado and Paul L. Owen et al. (New York: Bloomsbury T & T Clark, 2011), 115-116; Erik Larson (personal communication)).

[3] Burkett, *The Son of Man Debate*, 1-2.

[4] Darrell L. Bock, "The Use of Daniel 7 in Jesus' Trial, with Implications for his Self-Understanding," in *'Who is This Son of Man?': The Latest Scholarship on a Puzzling Expression of the Historical Jesus*, ed. Larry W. Hurtado and Paul L. Owen et al. (New York: Bloomsbury T & T Clark, 2011), 92.

of the phrase in antiquity. Nevertheless, many have seen the term as crucial in determining his self-understanding, given that it was used so exclusively and frequently by him.[5] If Jesus did use the term himself as a self-designation, examining it would perhaps allow one to gain more insight into Jesus' self-understanding.[6]

The first known interpretation of the designation of was given around 108 CE by the bishop Ignatius of Antioch, who viewed the expression as a title that underlined Jesus' human nature, whereas the title "Son of God" would be pointing out his divine nature.[7] At first glance, this seems like the most obvious and natural interpretation of the term for a Christian to make, and several of the early church fathers did have the same interpretation.[8] In the early 3rd century CE, Tertullian was the first to read Son of Man as a title that was derived from the passage in Daniel 7:13 in his work *Adversus Marcionem*:[9]

---

[5] Burkett, *The Son of Man Debate*, 1.

[6] Edward A. McDowell, *Son of Man and Suffering Servant: A Historical and Exegetical Study of Synoptic Narratives Revealing the Consciousness of Jesus Concerning His Person and Mission* (Tennessee: Broadman Press, 1946, 3rd printing), 96.

[7] Burkett, *The Son of Man Debate*, 7; Mogens Müller, *The Expression 'Son of Man' and the Development of Christology: A History of Interpretation* (Sheffield, UK: Equinox, 2012 paperback edition; "First published in hardback in 2008"), 12: Ignatius of Antioch indirectly interprets Son of Man as underlining Jesus' human nature in *Ephesians* 20:2 (*Ephesians* was a letter which was written by Ignatius).

[8] Daniel Boyarin, *The Jewish Gospels: The Story of the Jewish Christ* (New York: The New Press, 2012 (the paperback edition I used was published in 2013)), 25-26; Burkett, *The Son of Man Debate*, 7.

[9] Maurice Casey, *The Solution to the 'Son of Man' Problem* (New York: T & T Clark International, 2007), 99 of 6,420, Kindle edition. Several Kindle e-

> What now, if Christ be described in Daniel by this very title "Son of man?" Is not this enough to prove that He is the Christ of prophecy? For if He gives Himself that appellation which was provided in the prophecy for the Christ of the Creator, He undoubtedly offers Himself to be understood as Him to whom (the appellation) was assigned by the prophet.[10]

It was, however, the genealogical interpretation that became the most prevalent one early on and throughout the Middle Ages, and continued to be the most dominant one until the Protestant Reformation.[11] The fact that it was the most dominant view could be attributed to the fact that the early commentators relied only on the Greek form of the designation—transliterated as *ho huios tou anthropou*—without realizing that a Semitic phrase may have originally been behind the Greek.[12] The Greek term would be translated as "the man's son," making it seem as though Jesus were just saying he was the son of a certain parent or ancestor.[13] As to

---

books display no page number, therefore the location number was used instead in such cases.

[10] Tertullian, in "The Five Books Against Marcion," Book IV, Chapter X, Dr. Holmes, trans., in *Ante-Nicene Fathers Volume 3*, by Philip Schaff, ed. Allan Menzies (Michigan: Wm. B Eerdmans Publishing Co., originally published in 1885), 20,336 of 45,166, Kindle edition.

[11] Burkett, *The Son of Man Debate*, 3-4, 12.

[12] Geza Vermes, "The 'Son of Man' Debate," *Journal for the Study of the New Testament* no. 1 (October 1, 1978): 19, last accessed January 8, 2014, ATLA Religion Database with ATLASerials, EBSCOhost; Burkett, *The Son of Man Debate*, 12.

[13] Burkett, *The Son of Man Debate*, 6, 13.

whose son exactly, Burkett relates that two major options among scholars were Mary and Adam.[14] Mary could be a valid choice because "man" could be taken to mean "human being."[15] And by stressing the definite article, some offered that Jesus was *the* son or descendent of Adam, the promised seed that would be a source of blessing for many.[16] The genealogical interpretation was dominant enough in the Middle Ages that even some versions of the Bible would have "the son of the Virgin" written down in them instead of "the Son of Man."[17] However, from the 16th century onwards, the genealogical view grew increasingly out of favor, to the extent that by the 19th century the interpretation was virtually nonexistent.[18]

What precipitated this change was that in the 16th century exegetes came to realize that perhaps a Semitic expression lay behind the Greek one.[19] In Hebrew the designation is transliterated as *ben adam* (*adam* which can mean "man," "humankind," or "Adam"),[20] while in Aramaic it is transliterated as *bar enash* or *bar enasha*.[21] Once scholars realized that Jesus spoke not in Greek, but most probably in either Hebrew or Aramaic, the genealogical interpretation fell by the wayside.[22] In Hebrew or Aramaic, the expression

---

[14] Burkett, *The Son of Man Debate*, 3, 7-10.
[15] Ibid., 6.
[16] Ibid., 9-10.
[17] Ibid., 8.
[18] Ibid., 9.
[19] Ibid., 12-13; Vermes, "The 'Son of Man' Debate," 19.
[20] Bonnie Pedrotti Kittel, Victoria Hoffer, and Rebecca Abts Wright, *Biblical Hebrew Text and Workbook: Second Edition* (Connecticut: Yale University Press, 2005), 397.
[21] Vermes, "The 'Son of Man' Debate," 19.
[22] Burkett, *The Son of Man Debate*, 9.

would have only been another way of saying "man."[23] As a result, after the Protestant Reformation in the 16th century, several other interpretations were added to the genealogical one: the expression was interpreted as denoting merely his humanity (not in contrast to his divinity, but stressing his connection with the rest of humanity), or his "lowly humanity," stressing his connection specifically with the frailty and lowliness of human nature,[24] for many of the Son of Man sayings include Jesus' prediction of his imminent suffering and death. At the other end, some put forth that the term was describing Jesus as the "ideal" human because of the definite article, meaning that he was not just any human, but that he was the "ideal" human being, *the* human being "*par excellence.*"[25]

      Including the interpretations just given, there were three which either arose or became more prevalent in the 16th century: first, that the expression denoted Jesus' humanity (excluding the genealogical interpretation); second, that it was a Messianic title originating from Daniel 7:13; and third, that it was an idiomatic expression of self-reference.[26] Among the various interpretations, in the 16th and 17th centuries it was the interpretation that the term depicted Jesus' "lowly humanity" that was most widespread.[27] It was not until the 18th and 19th centuries that the interpretation that it was a Messianic title originating from Daniel became the most widespread, and remained so until the 1960s.[28]

---

[23] Burkett, *The Son of Man Debate*, 13.
[24] Ibid., 13-17.
[25] Ibid, 13.
[26] Ibid., 4.
[27] Ibid.
[28] Ibid., 23.

Coinciding with the quest for the historical Jesus that debuted in the 19th century, questions began to arise concerning the authenticity of the sayings and whether Jesus used the term to refer to himself.[29] In early 20th century, Rudolf Bultmann was one of the first to divide the sayings into three different categories, "which speak of the Son of Man (1) as coming, (2) as suffering death and rising again, and (3) as now at work."[30] Bultmann considered the Son of Man sayings belonging to the second category to be early church creations and that Son of Man was not used as a title in the sayings of the third category, but only as an idiomatic expression.[31] With regards to the first category, Bultmann argued that Jesus was not originally referring to himself when using the title of Son of Man, but to another future figure, and that it was the early church community that later identified Jesus with the Son of Man.[32]

Bultmann's students started the second quest for the historical Jesus in the 1960s (with the third quest following shortly) and soon many more scholars questioned the authenticity of the sayings, contending that they mostly originated with the early Christian community.[33] More recently, John Dominic Crossan, author of *The Historical Jesus: The Life of a Mediterranean Jewish Peasant*, came to the conclusion that nearly all of the Son of Man sayings were

---

[29] Burkett, *The Son of Man Debate*, 4, 31.
[30] Rudolf Bultmann, *Theology of the New Testament* (New York: Charles Scribner's Sons, 1951), 30.
[31] Ibid.
[32] Ibid., 9, 29-30.
[33] Darrell L. Bock, *Studying the Historical Jesus: A Guide to Sources and Methods* (Michigan: Baker Academic, 2002), 2,873 of 4,412, Kindle edition; Burkett, *The Son of Man Debate*, 31.

creations by the early church, with the exception of the saying found in Matthew 8:20 and Luke 9:58:[34] "Foxes have holes, and birds of the air have nests, but the Son of Man has nowhere to lay his head."[35]

The assessment that Son of Man was not a title, but a nontitular idiom of self-reference, also started to gain momentum towards the end of the 20th century, even though this view had been proposed as far back as the Reformation in the 16th century.[36] Vermes, for instance, was a proponent of the view that Jesus was indeed referring to himself, but that the Aramaic expression was not a title, but an idiom which Jesus used to refer to himself in a roundabout manner.[37] Scholarship went through two "Aramaic stages" in the 20th century (in the beginning of the 20th century and after World War II) during which scholars postulated that an Aramaic expression was underlying the Greek one.[38] Scholars started arriving at a consensus that Jesus spoke in Aramaic and that the Aramaic expression could possibly have been used in "three ways in the time of Jesus: (1) in the indefinite sense; (2) in the generic sense; and (3) in a titular or semi-titular sense."[39]

B. Methodology
1. Exegetical Method

---

[34] John Dominic Crossan, *The Historical Jesus: The Life of a Mediterranean Jewish Peasant* (Harper Collins e-books, 2010), 6,034-6,052 and 10,514-10,521 of 12,350, Kindle edition.

[35] Matthew 8:20.

[36] Burkett, *The Son of Man Debate*, 3-5, 81-82.

[37] Geza Vermes, *Jesus the Jew* (Pennsylvania: Fortress Press, 1973), 160-191.

[38] Müller, *The Expression 'Son of Man' and the Development of Christology*, 190.

[39] Ben Witherington, III, *The Christology of Jesus* (Minneapolis, Minnesota: Fortress Press, 1990), 237; Burkett, *The Son of Man Debate*, 5.

Although very few if any of the interpretations mentioned have completely disappeared, Burkett, in his book *The Son of Man Debate: A History and Evaluation* from 1999, considered that there were two main interpretations at the center of the debate at the time: "the apocalyptic/ messianic (in several variations) and the idiomatic/ nontitular (also in several variations)."[40] I will show that Jesus made the Son of Man into a Messianic title on the basis of the "son of man"[41] from the book of Daniel (specifically 7:13), an apocalyptic book from the *Tanakh* dated no later than the 2nd century BCE by scholars.[42] Although phrases and passages in the Bible may be polysemous, there are occasions in which one meaning is primary. The expression may arguably hold one primary interpretation, without thereby excluding all the others. As for the word "title," I will be using the following definition from the *New Oxford American Dictionary*: "A name that describes someone's position or job."[43] I will be relying on the scholarly research in the form of books and peer-reviewed articles. I will also be relying on Biblical commentaries. I will primarily be using the English Standard Version (hereafter referred to as ESV) of the Bible (of both the *Tanakh* and the New Testament) as my primary source. I will also be using some relevant ancient texts such as the apocalyptic texts of *The Similitudes of Enoch* (hereafter referred

---

[40] Burkett, *The Son of Man Debate*, 5.
[41] The English Standard Version (ESV) has "son of man" in Daniel 7:13 written with lowercase letters, while in the sayings of Jesus in the Gospels, "Son of Man" is written with capital letters.
[42] John J. Collins, *The Scepter and the Star: Messianism in the Light of the Dead Sea Scrolls* (Michigan and Cambridge, UK: Wm. B. Eerdmans Publishing Co., 2010), 43.
[43] *The New Oxford American Dictionary* (New York: Oxford University Press, Inc. e-book, 2010), 975,126 of 1,082,596, Kindle edition.

to as *Similitudes*) and *4 Ezra*. I will be carrying out the exegesis of the Son of Man sayings from the Gospel of Mark. "Son of Man" occurs 14 times in the Gospel, and there is a total of 13 Son of Man sayings in the Gospel, with two of them being in the form of indirect speech (Mark 8:31 and 9:9). The four Gospels represent the four earliest known written accounts of the life of Jesus, and I chose Mark in particular because it is generally agreed that it was the first one to be written and was one of the sources for Matthew and Luke. Thus its importance is unquestioned.

      I will be applying the methodological approach akin to the one Muslim scholar Amina Wadud-Musin uses for the Qur'an. Hers is a systematic three-fold exegetical approach that examines a given verse from historical-critical and philological perspectives, in addition to taking into account how the verse fits with the overall "spirit" of the Bible.[44] It is thus a holistic exegetical method that at first takes into account the wider historical and literary context behind a given verse or passage.[45] Second, it comprises a philological study of ambiguous words of a given verse, in order to eventually determine their origin and meaning in the context of the Bible.[46] Third, it implicates not taking a single verse in isolation, but understanding its relationship with the rest of the Bible.[47] A Son of Man saying will be examined both from an intratextual standpoint (looking at related passages within

---

[44] Amina Wadud, *Qur'an and Woman: Rereading the Sacred Text from a Woman's Perspective* (New York: Oxford University Press, 1999), 3-5, e-book last accessed March 3, 2019, ACLS Humanities E-book, http://hdl.handle.net/2027/heb.04755.
[45] Ibid.
[46] Ibid, 3, 5.
[47] Ibid.

Mark itself), as well as from an intertextual one (comparing with relevant passages from the rest of the Bible).[48] I will thus be reading Mark *vertically*, but also "*horizontally*, that is, across various accounts" in the Bible when relevant.[49] In addition, the narrative context of the pericope in which a saying occurs will also be taken into account in order to better assess its meaning.

2. Outline

In the chapter that follows, I will focus on the uses of appellation in the context of 1st century Judaism, concentrating mainly on Daniel 7, given the importance of the passage for interpreting what Jesus may have meant by the term. In the second part of the second chapter I will argue as to why "the Son of Man" was most probably uttered by Jesus himself (as were probably the allusions to the book of Daniel). The third chapter will be the actual exegesis of the sayings in the Gospel of Mark, and after establishing that it was used as a Messianic self-designation, the fourth and final chapter examines exactly what *type* of Messiah Jesus may have been referring to. Daniel Boyarin, in *The Jewish Gospels: The Story of the Jewish Christ*, has more recently argued that by identifying with the "son of man" in Daniel, Jesus was claiming to be not only a heavenly Messiah, but a divine one as well.[50] Boyarin stated how it is paradoxical that Jesus used

---

[48] Peter Müller, "Zwischen dem Gekommenen und dem Kommenden: Intertextuelle Aspekte der Menschensohnaussagen im Markusevangelium," in *Gottessohn und Menschesohn: Exegetische Studien zu Zwei Paradigmen Biblischer Intertextualität*, ed. Dieter Sänger, vol. 67 of *Biblisch-Theologische Studien*, ed. Jörg Frey et al. (Neukirchen-Vluyn, Germany: Neukirchener, 2004), 130.
[49] Bock, *Studying the Historical Jesus*, 4,243 of 4,412.
[50] Boyarin, *The Jewish Gospels*, 26, 31.

the designation to denote his divine nature, whereas many readers after Jesus have assumed that the term referred to his humanity.[51]

---

[51] Boyarin, *The Jewish Gospels*, 25-26, 30-31.

II. THE USE OF THE EXPRESSION AROUND JESUS' TIME
A. The Use of "Son of Man" Around Jesus' Time
1. Aramaic: Jesus' Native Language

The consensus among scholars is that Jesus spoke in Aramaic, though not necessarily in Aramaic alone.[1] Jesus also probably spoke Hebrew, at least when reading from Scriptures in the synagogues (as in Luke 4:18-19), and perhaps even Greek, for instance when he Jesus was conversing with the Roman prefect Pontius Pilate without the help of an interpreter.[2] He may have also needed to speak Greek on certain occasions when working as a carpenter.[3] In 1st century CE Israel, although the *Tanakh* was most probably read in Hebrew in the synagogues, Hebrew seems to have been less of a spoken tongue than Aramaic.[4] According to Gustaf Dalman, Aramaic was the first language of Galileans, a spoken language which could be comprehended as far as

---

[1] P. J. Williams, "Expressing Definiteness in Aramaic: A Response to Casey's Theory Concerning the Son of Man Sayings," in *'Who is This Son of Man?': The Latest Scholarship on a Puzzling Expression of the Historical Jesus*, ed. Larry W. Hurtado and Paul L. Owen et al. (New York: Bloomsbury T & T Clark, 2011), 66.

[2] Erik Larson (class notes); Ben Witherington, III, *The Christology of Jesus* (Minneapolis, Minnesota: Fortress Press, 1990), 236. Jesus could have also possibly been speaking in Latin with Pilate (Albert L. Lukaszewski, "Issues Concerning the Aramaic Behind ὁ Υἱὸς τοῦ ἀνθρώπου: A Critical Review of Scholarship," in *'Who is This Son of Man?': The Latest Scholarship on a Puzzling Expression of the Historical Jesus*, ed. Larry W. Hurtado and Paul L. Owen et al. (New York: Bloomsbury T & T Clark, 2011), 14).

[3] Didier Long, *Jésus de Nazareth, Juif de Galilée* (Paris, France: Presses de la Renaissance, 2011), 61.

[4] Lukaszewski, "Issues Concerning the Aramaic," 14.

Syria.[5] Not only was Jesus a Galilean, but his disciples were as well,[6] making Aramaic probably their "native tongue."[7] According to Maurice Casey, Aramaic was also the *lingua franca* of the Jews as a whole at the time.[8] And given that Jesus was Jewish and that he said that he "was sent only to the lost sheep of Israel"[9] (i.e., only to the Jews), he probably spoke Aramaic not only in Galilee, but throughout Israel. Jesus also gave special attention in his preaching to the poor, the ordinary, and the underprivileged; therefore it would have been more natural for Jesus to have reached out to them mainly in the language that was best understood by them.[10] According to Casey, Greek would have been less known by the underprivileged and Hebrew was a more literary, though sacred, language.[11] As a result, overall, it is highly probable

---

[5] Gustaf Dalman, *Words of Jesus Considered in the Light of Post-Biblical Jewish Writings and the Aramaic Language* (Edinburgh, Scotland: Morrison and Gibb Limited, 1902), 10, Google books.

[6] As indicated in Acts 2:7. Among the Twelve, it may be that only Judas Iscariot was not a Galilean (See John MacArthur, *Twelve Ordinary Men: How the Master Shaped His Disciples for Greatness and What He Wants to Do with You* (Nashville, Tennessee: Thomas Nelson, 2002), 149, Kindle edition).

[7] Craig A. Evans, *Fabricating Jesus: How Modern Scholars Distort the Gospels* (Illinois: Inter Varsity Press, 2006), 39, Kindle edition.

[8] Maurice Casey, "Aramaic Idiom and the Son of Man Problem: A Response to Owen and Shepherd," *Journal for the Study of the New Testament* 25, no. 1 (September 1, 2002): 5, last accessed January 22, 2014, ATLA Religion Database with ATLASerials, EBSCOhost; Maurice Casey, *The Solution to the 'Son of Man' Problem* (New York: T & T Clark International, 2007), 922 of 6,420, Kindle edition; Long, *Jésus de Nazareth, Juif de Galilée*, 58.

[9] Matthew 15:24.

[10] Dalman, *Words of Jesus*, 11.

[11] Lukaszewski, "Issues Concerning the Aramaic," 14.

that Jesus was speaking in Aramaic when he uttered his Son of Man sayings.

2. Use of "Son of Man" in the Tanakh

In the Hebrew Bible, there is not a single occurrence of "son of man" with the definite article. The only instance in Aramaic of the indefinite "son of man" is in Daniel 7:13 (a verse that will be examined in section B that follows in this chapter).[12] The other 105 instances of the indefinite "son of man" in the *Tanakh* are in Hebrew, a language which can be considered to be a "famous Semitic sister tongue" to Aramaic.[13] Yet even in Hebrew the use of the indefinite "son of man" is rare compared to that of "man" (*adam*).[14] In Hebrew, "son of man" (*ben adam*) occurs 105 times, while "man" (*adam*) occurs on 552 occasions, making "man" more than five times more frequent a term than "son of man." In the Hebrew Bible, the expression is mostly used to refer to a specific individual. The following table shows the various instances of the use of בן אדם (*ben adam*) in the *Tanakh* and in what sense they were used:[15]

---

[12] Adela Yarbro Collins and John J. Collins, *King and Messiah as Son of God: Divine, Human, and Angelic Messianic Figures in Biblical and Related Literature* (Michigan: Wm. B. Eerdmans Publishing Co., 2008), 160; Barnabas Lindars, *Jesus Son of Man: A Fresh Examination of the Son of Man Sayings in the Gospels in the Light of Recent Research* (Michigan: Wm. B. Eerdmans, 1983), 26.

[13] David Shepherd, "Re-Solving the Son of Man 'Problem' in Aramaic," in *"Who is This Son of Man?": The Latest Scholarship on a Puzzling Expression of the Historical Jesus*, ed. Larry W. Hurtado and Paul L. Owen et al. (New York: Bloomsbury T & T Clark, 2011), 59.

[14] Collins and Collins, *King and Messiah as Son of God*, 158.

[15] Data in table gathered using *Accordance*; verification that the underlying Hebrew expression was בן אדם (*ben adam*) using the Interlinear Bible in *Bible Hub*, last accessed April 26, 2019, biblehub.com/interlinear/. For example, the first result for "son of man" was in Numbers 23:19 in

Tanakh book	Number of instances in which בן אדם (ben adam) occurs	Employed in a sentence with a generic/indefinite meaning	Definite sense/ referring to a specific individual
Numbers	1	1	0
Job	3	3	0
Psalms	3	3	0
Isaiah	2	2	0
Jeremiah	2	2	0
Ezekiel	93	0	93
Daniel	1	0	1
Summary	105	11	94

As one can observe, "son of man" occurs 93 times in the book of Ezekiel.[16] Even though "son of man" occurs only in Hebrew in the book, Ezekiel the prophet is specifically addressed each time as "son of man" in definite statements solely addressing the prophet. In Daniel 8:17, the prophet Daniel is also addressed as "son of man" in Hebrew.[17] If even without the definite article, *ben adam* could be used in definite statements, there is no reason as to why the equivalent expression in Aramaic could not do likewise. As the Hebrew Bible features no "son of man" with the

---

Accordance, and then using the Interlinear Bible, I verified that *ben adam* was the underlying expression ("Numbers 23:19," *Bible Hub*, last accessed May 25, 2015, http://biblehub.com/interlinear/numbers/23-19.htm). Unless explicitly stated otherwise, the Interlinear Bible was used to view the underlying Hebrew, Greek, or Aramaic.

[16] *Accordance*.

[17] José Ramón Scheifler, "El Hijo del Hombre en Daniel," *Estudios Eclesiásticos* 34, no. 134-135 (July 1, 1960): 791, last accessed January 22, 2014, ATLA Religion Database with ATLASerials, EBSCOhost.

definite article, it is not surprising that there is no occurrence with the definite article in the LXX, the 2nd century BCE Greek translation of the *Tanakh*; but the indefinite occurrences are faithfully translated.[18]

3. Use of "Son of Man" Before and During the Time of Jesus

a. The Extant Occurrences

With *bar enasha*, Jesus uttered an "unusual and distinctive Aramaic expression."[19] There is no known instance of "son of man" in Aramaic with the definite article in any text dating from before Jesus.[20] "*The* Son of Man" was thus practically unheard of in history until Jesus himself frequently used the expression.[21]

In Aramaic, even the indefinite form was rare, as there are only five examples of the indefinite expression being

---

[18] Hurtado, "Summary and Concluding Observations," 160.
[19] Ibid., 174.
[20] Collins and Collins, *King and Messiah as Son of God*, 160; Joseph A. Fitzmyer, "Another View of the 'Son of Man' Debate," *Journal for the Study of the New Testament* no. 4 (July 1, 1979): 65, last accessed November 10, 2013, ATLA Religion Database with ATLASerials, EBSCOhost; Hurtado, "Summary and Concluding Observations," 167; Paul Owen, and David Shepherd, "Speaking Up for Qumran, Dalman and the Son of Man: Was Bar Enasha a Common Term for 'Man' in the Time of Jesus?" *Journal for the Study of the New Testament* no. 81 (March 1, 2001): 120-121, last accessed January 18, 2014, ATLA Religion Database with ATLASerials, EBSCOhost.
[21] Hurtado, "Summary and Concluding Observations," 162.

used before the time of Jesus (even including instances from the 1st century CE).[22] They are shown in the following table:[23]

Text/Inscription	Number of instances in which בר אנש (*bar enash*) occurs	Employed in a generic/indefinite sense	Definite sense/ referring to a specific individual
Sefire III.14-16	1	1	0
Daniel 7:13	1	?	?
Qumran texts	3	3	0
Summary	5	4 (5?)	0 (the *bar enash* in Daniel may be the exception)

The instance found in the *Sefire* inscriptions is the earliest one, dating from around 750 BCE.[24] The Dead Sea Scrolls contain three instances of *bar enash*, from texts dating anywhere from the 2nd century BCE to around 68 CE.[25] *Bar enash* has a generic or indefinite sense in the occasions in

---

[22] Casey, "Aramaic Idiom and the Son of Man Problem," 27-30; Owen and Shepherd, "Speaking Up for Qumran, Dalman, and the Son of Man," 107-119.

[23] Data in table gathered from Casey, *The Solution to the 'Son of Man' Problem*, and from *'Who is This Son of Man?': The Latest Scholarship on a Puzzling Expression of the Historical Jesus*, ed. Larry W. Hurtado and Paul L. Owen et al. (New York: Bloomsbury T & T Clark, 2011).

[24] Casey, *The Solution to the 'Son of Man' Problem*, 916 of 6420.

[25] Lukaszewski, "Issues Concerning the Aramaic," 21.

which it occurs, with the only possible exception being in Daniel 7:13, which will be discussed shortly.

b. Reconstruction of "the Son of Man" into Aramaic

In order to determine what the exact form of the expression Jesus was using, the most relevant texts are the Aramaic texts from Qumran, for, according to P.J. Williams, "we are either faced with the small corpus of Aramaic among the Dead Sea Scrolls, inscriptions and contemporary documents, or we have to use sources from considerably later."[26] The ancient texts which are closest in time and in geography to the Aramaic of 1st century Galilee are thus the Dead Sea Scrolls, which date from approximately 200 BCE to 68 CE.[27] It is the general consensus among scholars that the Aramaic texts from the Dead Sea Scrolls are the best sources for attempting to reconstruct Jesus' Aramaic sayings from the Greek New Testament.[28] Although the expression with the definite article (with the Aramaic equivalent of "the") is absent from the Qumran documents, the Dead Sea Scrolls do contain the indefinite "son of man" and definite and indefinite forms of "sons of men." The indefinite "sons of men" occurs in *1QapGen* 19:15, while the definite "sons of men" occurs in *11QarJob* 13:9 and 28:2, *4QenAst* 23:1, and *1QapGen* 6:8-9.[29] The indefinite "son of man" occurs in *11QarJob* 9:9, 26:3, and in *1QapGen* 21:13:[30]

---

[26] Williams, "Expressing Definiteness in Aramaic," 67.
[27] Lukaszewski, "Issues Concerning the Aramaic," 21.
[28] Casey, "Aramaic Idiom and the Son of Man Problem," 31; Casey, *The Solution to the 'Son of Man' Problem*, 930 of 6,420; Lukaszewski, "Issues Concerning the Aramaic," 26.
[29] Shepherd, "Re-Solving the Son of Man 'Problem' in Aramaic," 50.
[30] Ibid.

> How much less a mortal, a maggot, and a s]on
> of man, a wor[m!³¹
> Your sin [affects a man like yo]u, and your
> righteousness a son of man.³²
> And I will multiply your seed like the dust of
> the earth which no son of man can count.³³

From the basis of the Aramaic texts and fragments from the Dead Sea Scrolls, there are several possible ways of writing the construct of the Aramaic expression underlying the Greek phrase of the New Testament:

1. בר אנשא (*bar enasha*): "The Son of Man."
2. בר אנש (*bar enash*): "Son of Man."
3. ברא אנשא (*bara enasha*): "The Son of Man."
4. בר די אנש (*bar di enash*): "The Son of Man."
5. בר די אנשא (*bar di enasha*): "The Son of Man."
6. ברה די אנש (*bareh di enash*): "The Son of Man."³⁴

Of the various ways of writing a construct chain, the first two choices represent the most common way of writing

---

³¹ *11QarJob* 9:9 (Casey, *The Solution to the 'Son of Man' Problem*, 1,043 of 6,420).
³² *11QarJob* 26:2-3 (Casey, *The Solution to the 'Son of Man' Problem*, 1,045 of 6,420).
³³ *1QapGen* 21:13 (Casey, *The Solution to the 'Son of Man' Problem*, 1,002 of 6,420).
³⁴ Lukaszewski, "Issues Concerning the Aramaic," 23. Lukaszewski lists seven possibilities, but two of them are the same as the fourth possibility, except that in one case *bar* would be in the absolute form and in the other in the construct form.

it in the Dead Sea Scrolls.³⁵ The first two options have thus been proposed the most often by modern scholars for the actual expression Jesus used. ³⁶ Given that (1) the constructs in options 1 and 2 are the most common in Qumran; and (2) close to 96% do not have the relative particle די as in the examples 4, 5, and 6, it is reasonable to assume that Jesus most likely used the form of בר אנש(א) (*bar enash(a)*).³⁷ For my thesis, it is not necessary to choose any one form of the expression over another, but to simplify the matter it seems best to assume that it was of the form of בר אנש(א).

In the Greek Gospels, Jesus pronounces the phrase each and every time with the definite article, with the only exception being in John 5:27, which lacks the definite article but is nevertheless evidently referring to Jesus exclusively.³⁸ If the Greek translation is consistent with the underlying Aramaic expression that Jesus uttered, then Jesus also continually used the definite form in Aramaic rather than the indefinite one.³⁹ Consequently, as David Shepherd states, "the articular form of the Greek expression found on the lips of Jesus in the New Testament is best explained as a faithful translation of his use of the singular" definite בר אנשא (*bar enasha*).⁴⁰

---

³⁵ Lukaszewski, "Issues Concerning the Aramaic," 24.
³⁶ Ibid.
³⁷ Ibid.
³⁸ Benjamin E. Reynolds, "The Use of the Son of Man Idiom in the Gospel of John," in *'Who is This Son of Man?': The Latest Scholarship on a Puzzling Expression of the Historical Jesus*, ed. Larry W. Hurtado and Paul L. Owen et al. (New York: Bloomsbury T & T Clark, 2011), 115-116.
³⁹ Delbert Burkett, *The Son of Man Debate: A History and Evaluation*, (Cambridge, UK: Cambridge University Press, 1999), 92-93.
⁴⁰ Shepherd, "Re-Solving the Son of Man 'Problem' in Aramaic," 60; Larry W. Hurtado, "Summary and Concluding Observations," in *'Who is*

4. Use of "Son of Man" in Later Jewish Literature

After Qumran, the next texts that are closest to Jesus' time in which the expression occurs in Aramaic are the Targum Onkelos (to the Torah) and the Targum Jonathan (to the Prophets), that scholars date to before the end of the 2nd century CE.[41] However, there is no instance of the definite expression in the Targum Onkelos.[42] The two only examples of the definite form are found in the Targum Jonathan to the *Nevi'im* (which are also the only extant Aramaic examples of the definite form in the period of 200 BCE to 200CE).[43] In *Jonathan*, in Isaiah 56:2 and 51:12, the indefinite phrase in Hebrew is translated to Aramaic with a definite expression.[44] In both cases it does not refer to a particular individual, but, apart from these two examples, the definite form is absent in the Targums.[45]

Given that the definite phrase is virtually nonexistent in extant Aramaic texts around the time of Jesus, modern scholars have had to rely mainly on later sources to posit how

---

This Son of Man?': The Latest Scholarship on a Puzzling Expression of the Historical Jesus, ed. Larry W. Hurtado and Paul L. Owen et al. (New York: Bloomsbury T & T Clark, 2011), 174.

[41] Shepherd, "Re-Solving the Son of Man 'Problem' in Aramaic," 53. A Targum is "any of several translations of the Hebrew Bible or portions of it into the Aramaic language. The word originally indicated a translation of the Old Testament in any language but later came to refer specifically to an Aramaic translation" (*Encyclopædia Britannica*, "Targum (Biblical Literature)," last accessed March 26, 2019,
http://www.britannica.com/EBchecked/topic/583515/Targum).

[42] Shepherd, "Re-Solving the Son of Man 'Problem' in Aramaic," 54.

[43] Ibid., 56.

[44] Ibid.

[45] Ibid., 57; Owen and Shepherd, "Speaking Up for Qumran, Dalman and the Son of Man," 120-121.

it was possibly used.[46] On the basis of those later texts, scholars have postulated that "son of man" was used idiomatically in three different ways: that "son of man" was used in 1st century Galilee as a generic term for "man," in a non-specific sense ("a man" or "any man"), or as a circumlocution for "I."[47]

Casey is of the view that the expression could only be used with a generic meaning, although it could be used when referring to a specific individual.[48] He did not rely solely on later texts, but postulated his theory also on the texts pre-dating Jesus and the Dead Sea Scrolls. In later Jewish literature, the Babylonian and Palestinian Talmuds (as well as the Jewish *midrashim*) contain some examples of the definite בר אנשא being used to make generic statements.[49] Casey also postulated that because he considered *bar (e)nash(a)* to only have a generic meaning, the definite article in Aramaic would have made no difference in the sayings of Jesus.[50]

The examples provided by Casey show that the expression could be used in a generic way, but they only show that it could be used in that manner, not that it could not be used in other ways.[51] The 1st century CE Jewish apocalyptic

---

[46] Shepherd, "Re-Solving the Son of Man 'Problem' in Aramaic," 51-52.
[47] Burkett, *The Son of Man Debate*, 82.
[48] Casey, *The Solution to the 'Son of Man' Problem*, 964 and 1,071 of 6,420.
[49] Paul L. Owen, "Problems with Casey's 'Solution'," in *'Who is This Son of Man?': The Latest Scholarship on a Puzzling Expression of the Historical Jesus*, ed. Larry W. Hurtado and Paul L. Owen et al. (New York: Bloomsbury T & T Clark, 2011), 31; Richard Bauckham, "The Son of Man: 'A Man in my Position' or 'Someone,'" *Journal for the Study of the New Testament* no. 23 (February 1, 1985): 27, last accessed January 10, 2014, ATLA Religion Database with ATLASerials, EBSCOhost.
[50] Casey, *The Solution to the 'Son of Man' Problem*, 961 of 6,420.
[51] Witherington, *The Christology of Jesus*, 246.

text called the *Similitudes*, which according to Casey was originally written in Aramaic,[52] *does* show that the definite expression was used in a non-generic sense, with the definite article serving to refer to a specific individual, who is even identified as the Messiah.[53] The very purpose of the definite article is to point to a specified person or object, and Jesus perhaps deliberately chose the definite form precisely for that reason. And as will be shown in the third chapter, Jesus never used the expression in generic statements, but only in definite ones that could only be applied to him.

Vermes contended that בר נשא was indeed used to refer exclusively to the speaker, though in a roundabout manner, by using generic statements that created a *double entendre*.[54] Yet Vermes argued that it could not be used as a title, but could only be used only as a circumlocution for "I" when "the speaker may wish to refrain from immodest emphasis on himself," and when making statements that are of a "unpleasant, frightening or fateful nature," especially those involving the topics of "sickness and death."[55] It may be true that also around the time of Jesus it was perhaps not uncommon for someone to suddenly speak in the third person so as to not appear boastful or when involving the fearful subject such as death.[56] At least there is one such

---

[52] Casey, *The Solution to the 'Son of Man' Problem*, 1,566 of 6,420.
[53] Ibid., 505 of 6,420; John J. Collins, *The Scepter and the Star: Messianism in the Light of the Dead Sea Scrolls* (Michigan and Cambridge, UK: Wm. B. Eerdmans Publishing Co., 2010), 203; Howard Clarke Kee, "Christology in Mark's Gospel," *Judaisms and Their Messiahs at the Turn of the Christian Era*, ed. Jacob Neusner et al. (New York: Cambridge University Press, 1987), 191.
[54] Vermes, *Jesus the Jew*, 165.
[55] Ibid., 163.
[56] Ibid.

example in the New Testament, pointed out by Vermes,[57] in which the Apostle Paul refers to himself in roundabout fashion by using the indefinite expression "a man":

> I know a man in Christ who fourteen years ago was caught up to the third heaven—whether in the body or out of the body I do not know, God knows. And I know that this man was caught up into paradise—whether in the body or out of the body I do not know, God knows—and he heard things that cannot be told, which man may not utter. On behalf of this man I will boast, but on my own behalf I will not boast, except of my weaknesses—though if I should wish to boast, I would not be a fool, for I would be speaking the truth; but I refrain from it, so that no one may think more of me than he sees in me or hears from me.[58]

It is clear from the example that Paul switches to the indefinite and demonstrative expressions ("a man" and "this man") in order to not appear boastful. The expression of *bar enasha* may have been used as an idiom of self-reference, but that would not have prevented Jesus from using it as a title as well.[59] Like Paul, Jesus could have chosen "man" if he wanted

---

[57] Geza Vermes, *The Changing Faces of Jesus* (New York: Penguin Books, 2000), 294-295.
[58] 2 Corinthians 12:2-6.
[59] Alejandro Díez Macho, "La Cristología del Hijo del Hombre y el Uso de la Tercera Persona en Vez de la Primera," *Scripta Theologica* 14, no. 1

to speak in a roundabout manner, and he could have also chosen "man" to express a generic meaning.[60] Yet he chose a designation in Aramaic that was even rare in its indefinite form before his coming, which suggests that he chose it for something other than to use it idiomatically.[61] For instance, the Jerusalem Talmud contains the following statement in *Ta'anith* 2.1 65b,[62] from the late 3rd century CE Rabbi Abbahu: "If a man says to you, 'I am (a) God,' he is a liar; 'I am (a) Son of Man,' he will regret it; 'I go up to heaven,' he has said it but he will not be able to do it.'"[63] This seems to precisely be paraphrasing Jesus' response in Mark 14:62.[64] Although the example is in Hebrew, it shows not only that the speaker is referring solely to himself even without the definite article, but also that the "son of man" is not merely

---

(January 1, 1982): 189, last accessed January 22, 2014, ATLA Religion Database with ATLASerials, EBSCOhost.

[60] For instance, in Mark 2:27, Jesus used "man" to make a generic statement.

[61] Idea from Fitzmyer, "Another View of the 'Son of Man' Debate," 65; cf. Morna Dorothy Hooker, "Is the Son of Man Problem Really Insoluble?" In *Text and Interpretation: Studies in the New Testament Presented to Matthew Black*, ed. Ernest Best and R.McL. Wilson (Cambridge, UK: Cambridge University Press, 1979), 157.

[62] Jacob Neusner, *The Talmud of the Land of Israel: An Academic Commentary to the Second, Third, and Fourth Divisions: VIII. Yerushalmi Tractate Taanit* (Georgia, USA: Scholars Press, 1998), 41; Craig L. Blomberg, *Jesus and the Gospels: An Introduction and Survey* (Nashville, Tennessee: B&H Publishing Group, 2009), 12,881 of 14,489, Kindle edition; Robert M. Bowman Jr. and J. Ed Komoszewski, *Putting Jesus in His Place: The Case for the Deity of Christ* (Michigan: Kregel Publications, 2007), 4,145 of 4,522, Kindle edition

[63] Blomberg, *Jesus and the Gospels*, 12,881 of 14,489.

[64] Bowman and Komoszewski, *Putting Jesus in His Place*, 2,800 of 4,522.

taken as a generic or circumlocutional idiom,[65] or R. Abbahu would not state that the speaker would "regret" saying it.

Another possibility is that Jesus used the phrase to refer to a "son of man" from the *Tanakh*, particularly the "son of man" in Daniel 7:13.[66] Outside the New Testament, there are several contemporary texts (in addition to *Similitudes*) that allude to the "son of man" of Daniel 7:13 (and other verses from Daniel).

B. Daniel and Apocalyptic Literature
1. Daniel: The Apocalyptic Book of the Bible

Before examining the ancient texts from around the time of Jesus that relied on Daniel, it is important to first focus on the passage of Daniel 7 itself, which is so crucial for the interpretation of Jesus' use of the designation. The dates given by scholars for Daniel's time of writing vary widely, but the ones presented by modern scholars are not any later than the second century BCE, for fragments of Daniel that were found in Qumran date as early as that time.[67] Collins also affirms that Daniel "shows no Roman influence," confirming the view that the book could not have been written any later than the 2nd century BCE.[68] According to the *Tanakh*, however, the prophet Daniel had the vision of chapter 7 during the beginning of king Belshazzar's reign (who ruled Babylon with Nabodinus),[69] which would have been during

---

[65] Shepherd, "Re-Solving the Son of Man 'Problem' in Aramaic," 60.
[66] Hurtado, "Summary and Concluding Observations," 175.
[67] Collins, *The Scepter and the Star*, 43.
[68] Ibid.; Daniel Boyarin, *The Jewish Gospels: The Story of the Jewish Christ* (New York: The New Press, 2012 (the paperback edition I used was published in 2013)), 31.
[69] *NLT Parallel Study Bible* (Illinois: Tyndale House Publishers, Inc., 2011), 1,549.

the Babylonian Exile, around 556-553 BCE.[70] Daniel first sees four beasts in his vision, each beast representing a different ruler or worldly power that would successively be defeated before the appearance of the "son of man."[71] The interpretation of what the fourth beast symbolizes varies.[72] The fourth beast could thus represent the coming into power of a ruler of the Roman Empire, or perhaps Antiochus IV Epiphanes, who oppressed the Jews in the 2nd century BCE by attempting to ban both circumcision and the reading of Scriptures.[73] The saints inheriting the kingdom in Daniel 7 would then represent the Maccabean saints.[74] Yet the fourth beast is implicitly interpreted as the Roman Empire in the 1st century CE apocalyptic texts of *4 Ezra* and *2 Baruch*.[75] What seems clear however is that "the fourth beast is of a unique character (7.19), and significance (cf. 7.7-8, 19-21)."[76]

    The beginning and ending of the book of Daniel is in Hebrew, but the middle chapters are in Aramaic (chapters 2 to 7).[77] Some scholars have argued that the whole book was originally written in Hebrew and chapters 2-7 were only later

---

[70] Daniel 7:1.

[71] Owen, "Problems with Casey's 'Solution'," 35-36.

[72] Ibid., 35.

[73] Erik Larson (class notes); Vermes, *Jesus the Jew*, 169; John Dominic Crossan, *The Historical Jesus: The Life of a Mediterranean Jewish Peasant* (Harper Collins e-books, 2010), 5,643 of 12,350, Kindle edition.

[74] See Norman Perrin, "Son of Man in Ancient Judaism and Primitive Christianity: A Suggestion" *Biblical Research* 11, (January 1, 1966): 20, last accessed January 22, 2014, ATLA Religion Database with ATLASerials, EBSCOhost.

[75] Long, Didier, *L'Invention du Christianisme: Et Jésus Devint Dieu* (Paris, France: Presses de la Renaissance, 2012), 108.

[76] Owen, "Problems with Casey's 'Solution'," 35.

[77] *NLT Parallel Study Bible*, 1,535.

translated into Aramaic. But the point at which the switch is made from Hebrew to Aramaic (Daniel 2:4) is preserved in the Danielic fragments from Qumran, and the change is exactly as it is in the Masoretic text. This means that that Daniel 7 was already in Aramaic before the coming of Jesus.[78] The following quotation is from the crucial passage of Daniel 7:13-14:

> I saw in the night visions, and behold, with the clouds of heaven there came one like a son of man, and he came to the Ancient of Days and was presented before him. And to him was given dominion and glory and a kingdom, that all peoples, nations and languages should serve him; his dominion is an everlasting dominion, which shall not pass away, and his kingdom one that shall not be destroyed.

Modern scholars are divided over the interpretation of the Danielic "son of man." Two major interpretations regarding the "son of man" are: (1) that the "son of man" is merely symbolic, representing the people of Israel; and (2) that the "son of man" is an individual.[79] A third major

---

[78] *NLT Parallel Study Bible*, 1,535.
[79] Julian Morgenstern, "'Son of Man' of Daniel 7:13f: A New Interpretation." *Journal Of Biblical Literature* 80, no. 1 (March 1, 1961): 65, last accessed January 22, 2014, ATLA Religion Database with ATLASerials, EBSCOhost; Scheifler, "El Hijo del Hombre en Daniel," 789.

interpretation is that the figure is an angelic being,[80] but whether the figure is an angel or not is not very problematic for my thesis, but whether the figure is an individual or not is.[81] Both interpretations can be gathered from the passage, but on the face of it, it does seem that the "one like a son of man" symbolizes the Israelites collectively when an angel interprets Daniel's vision. When giving the prophet Daniel its interpretation, the angel says the following:

> But the saints of the Most High shall receive the kingdom and possess the kingdom forever, forever and ever.[82]
> [T]he Ancient of Days came, and judgment was given for the saints of the Most High, and the time came when the saints possessed the kingdom.[83]
> And the kingdom and the dominion and the greatness of the kingdoms under the whole heaven shall be given to the people of the saints of the Most High; his kingdom shall be

---

[80] Edward Adams, "The Coming of the Son of Man in Mark's Gospel," *Tyndale Bulletin* 56, no. 2 (January 1, 2005): 44, last accessed January 10, 2014, ATLA Religion Database with ATLASerials, EBSCOhost; Lindars, *Jesus Son of Man*, 10; Mogens Müller, *The Expression 'Son of Man' and the Development of Christology: A History of Interpretation* (Sheffield, UK: Equinox, 2012 paperback edition; "First published in hardback in 2008"), 335.
[81] It will not be very problematic either when I will argue that the Danielic figure is divine, but in that case the "son of man" could not be just any angel, but would have to be *the* Angel of the LORD.
[82] Daniel 7:18.
[83] Daniel 7:22.

an everlasting kingdom, and all dominions
shall serve and obey him.[84]

There is, however, sufficient ambiguity in Daniel's vision that makes it difficult to decide whether he is an individual or not. This may be because of the fact that in antiquity the difference between a king and his kingdom was not always clearly distinguished.[85] Even in the vision of the beasts in Daniel 7, the fourth beast may be interpreted either way, for the fourth beast is said to be both a king (7:17) and a kingdom (7:23). Yet the first beast in 7:4 probably represents specifically King Nebuchadnezzar, who "had taken on the mind of a beast (4:16, 32, 33), but then was restored and learned to acknowledge the Most High God."[86] What all scholars seem to agree on is that the "son of man" is a positive figure. He stands in contrast to the beasts of the other kingdoms.[87]

There are nonetheless several factors that would lead one to interpret him as an individual. In chapter 5 of Daniel, a chapter also in Aramaic, the prophet Daniel tells King Belshazzar, "Your kingdom is divided and given to the Medes and Persians."[88] Yet Daniel 5:30 explicitly states that "Darius the Mede received the kingdom, being about sixty-two years old." In the same way, despite the fact that the Israelites

---

[84] Daniel 7:27.
[85] Witherington, *The Christology of Jesus*, 239.
[86] *NLT Parallel Study Bible*, 1,549.
[87] S.E. Johnson, "Son of Man," In *Interpreter's Dictionary of the Bible*, Volume 4 (New York/ Tennessee: Abingdon Press, 1962), 414; Robert D. Rowe, "Is Daniel's 'Son of Man' Messianic?" In *Christ the Lord: Studies in Christology presented to Donald Guthrie*, ed. Harold H. Rowdon (Leicester, UK: Inter-Varsity Press, 1982), 88.
[88] Daniel 5:28.

"shall receive the kingdom,"⁸⁹ they would nonetheless have a king over them,⁹⁰ in this case perhaps the Danielic "son of man." With regards to the "son of man," Daniel 7:14 states that "all peoples, nations, and languages should serve him." Given that the verse states "all ... nations," the nation of Israel would evidently be one of them.⁹¹ Perhaps the Israelites only receive the kingdom because the "son of man," the one to whom the kingdom belongs, shares it with them.⁹²

      The individual interpretation of the Danielic "son of man" is also favored by the earliest interpretations of the text in writings from around the time of Jesus.⁹³ The collective interpretation was held early on,⁹⁴ but according to John J. Collins, it was not until R. Ibn Ezra (c. 1060 to c. 1139 CE) that the interpretation of the "son of man" as a symbol for the people of Israel was explicitly mentioned in any Jewish text.⁹⁵ In addition, all the earliest interpretations identified the Danielic "son of man" with the Messiah.⁹⁶ *Similitudes* and *4 Ezra* were the first two Jewish texts to allude to Daniel 7 and (at least indirectly) to the "son of man" figure.⁹⁷ However,

---

[89] Daniel 7:18.
[90] Rowe, "Is Daniel's 'Son of Man' Messianic?" 95.
[91] Owen, "Problems with Casey's 'Solution'," 37.
[92] Ibid.
[93] Burkett, *The Son of Man Debate*, 23.
[94] For instance, the corporate interpretation is mentioned in a 4th century CE text attributed to the Christian theologian Ephraem (Casey, *The Solution to the 'Son of Man' Problem*, 1,397-1,404 of 6,420).
[95] Collins, *The Scepter and the Star*, 211; *Encyclopædia Britannica*, "Moses Ibn Ezra," last accessed April 23, 2019, http://www.britannica.com/EBchecked/topic/280743/Moses-ibn-Ezra.
[96] Burkett, *The Son of Man Debate*, 119; Collins and Collins, *King and Messiah as Son of God*, 79.
[97] Collins, *The Scepter and the Star*, 188.

already in Qumran, two apocalyptic texts were found in which the book of Daniel was used in depicting an eschatological figure.

2. The Qumran Literature

The Qumranic *Son of God* text, or *4Q246* (also called the *Aramaic Apocalypse*), was probably written sometime in the 1st century BCE.[98] Daniel 7:13 is not directly quoted, but allusions to Daniel are sufficiently explicit for the text to have at one point been called *4QpseudoDaniel*.[99] The most unambiguous allusions to Daniel in the Qumran text occur at 2:5 and 2:9.[100] In 2:5 the text states, "Their (the people of God's) kingdom will be an eternal kingdom,"[101] which closely matches Daniel 4:3 or 7:27.[102] In 2:9, it is stated, "Their dominion will be an eternal dominion,"[103] which is similar to the statements in Daniel 4:34 and 7:14.[104] Many interpretations have been given concerning the "Son of God" figure depicted in the text, and there is debate even over whether he is a good or evil figure, but according to Adela Yarbro Collins and John J. Collins, it is probable that most scholars are of the view that he is a good one, and a Messianic one as well.[105] The figure is called both "Son of God" and "son of the Most High," just as Jesus is in Luke

---

[98] Geza Vermes, trans., *The Complete Dead Sea Scrolls in English* (London, UK/ New York: Penguin Books, 2011, 5th ed.), 11,476 of 13,411, Kindle edition.
[99] Collins and Collins, *King and Messiah as Son of God*, 69.
[100] Ibid.; Collins, *The Scepter and the Star*, 176.
[101] Vermes, *The Complete Dead Sea Scrolls in English*, 11,494 of 13,411.
[102] Collins, *The Scepter and the Star*, 176.
[103] Vermes, *The Complete Dead Sea Scrolls in English*, 11,501 of 13,411.
[104] Collins, *The Scepter and the Star*, 176.
[105] Ibid., 174; Collins and Collins, *King and Messiah as Son of God*, 66.

1:32, 35.[106] Thus not only is the figure in *4Q246* widely interpreted by scholars as a positive and Messianic one, but the very same titles of "Son of the Most High" and "Son of God" were later used to refer to Jesus. If the author of *4Q246* was depicting a Messianic figure, then *4Q246* was arguably the first text in the Hellenistic period (323 BCE to 30 BCE) to express the expectation for a Davidic Messiah.[107] The "Son of God" text would also have been the first text to allude to Daniel 7 (even if in a circuitous manner) when depicting a Messianic figure.[108] In *4Q246*, it also states that "all provinces will pay homage to them,"[109] a phrase which can also be translated as "all cities will pay him [or it] homage."[110] If it was the author's intent for the "homage" to be addressed to the Messianic figure alone, then the text is depicting a figure that is also possibly divine.

Another important Dead Sea Scrolls text which alludes to Daniel when depicting an eschatological figure is *11Q Melchizedek* (or *11Q13*).[111] The text, from around 1st century BCE,[112] presents what seems to be a highly exalted heavenly authority with a redeeming role.[113] The text depicts a Messianic figure who will come to *"comfort all who mourn, to*

---

[106] Collins, *The Scepter and the Star*, 172.
[107] Ibid., 188; *Encyclopædia Britannica*, "Hellenistic Age (Ancient Greek History)," last accessed April 23, 2019,
http://www.britannica.com/EBchecked/topic/260307/Hellenistic-Age.
[108] Collins, *The Scepter and the Star*, 188.
[109] Vermes, *The Complete Dead Sea Scrolls in English*, 11,501 of 13,411.
[110] Collins, *The Scepter and the Star*, 172.
[111] Vermes, *The Complete Dead Sea Scrolls in English*, 10,351 of 13,411.
[112] Ibid.
[113] Ibid., 10, 356 of 13,411; Collins and Collins, *King and Messiah as Son of God*, 80.

grant to those who mourn in Zion."[114] In *11Q13*, Daniel is also referenced: "and *the messenger* is the Anointed one of the spirit, concerning whom Dan[iel] said …"[115] According to Bock, the verse is probably specifically alluding to Daniel 9:25,[116] which refers to "the coming of an anointed one, a prince." Like the Messianic figure in the "Son of God" text, Melchizedek is given a highly exalted, if not divine, status, and is given the role of judgment.[117]

3. The Similitudes of Enoch

The book of Enoch consists of five sections, one of which is *Similitudes* or the *Book of Parables of Enoch*. At Qumran, *Similitudes* is conspicuously absent, for Aramaic fragments were found for each of the books of Enoch except *Similitudes*.[118] This had led some scholars to conclude that the *Similitudes* book was written after the others, which would be after 68 CE, given that the site of Qumran was inhabited as late as 68 CE. The only one to quote any of the Enochic books in the New Testament is Jude, Jesus' half brother, who in the Letter attributed to him included a quotation from Enoch 1:9 in verses 14 and 15, but none from *Similitudes*. Overall, however, "no contemporary *Parables'* scholar would

---

[114] Vermes, *The Complete Dead Sea Scrolls in English*, 10,382 of 13,411.
[115] Ibid.
[116] Darrell L. Bock, "The Use of Daniel 7 in Jesus' Trial, with Implications for his Self-Understanding," in *'Who is This Son of Man?': The Latest Scholarship on a Puzzling Expression of the Historical Jesus*, ed. Larry W. Hurtado and Paul L. Owen et al. (New York: Bloomsbury T & T Clark, 2011), 85; Collins and Collins, *King and Messiah as Son of God*, 80-83.
[117] Collins and Collins, *King and Messiah as Son of God*, 85; David Flusser, *Jesus* (Jerusalem: The Hebrew University Press, 2001), 5088 of 8469, Kindle edition.
[118] Burkett, *The Son of Man Debate*, 70; Lindars, *Jesus Son of Man*, 5; Müller, *The Expression 'Son of Man' and the Development of Christology*, 337.

stray outside of the years 34 BC to AD 135."[119] Evidence suggests that it was originally written in Hebrew or Aramaic, but "either way, we stand at two removes from that original Semitic text of the *Parables*," which today is available in complete form only in Ethiopic.[120] It is also possible that a few interpolations found their way into the text after it was originally written.[121]

In *Similitudes*, there are 14 instances of either "the Son of Man" or "that Son of Man" in the Ethiopic version of the text. In addition to the expression "Son of Man," the prophet's vision from Daniel 7 is referred to and interpreted in chapters 46 and 47 of *Similitudes*.[122] The following passage from 46:1-2 of *Similitudes* mentions a "Son of Man" that accompanies "the Head of Days," an obvious allusion to Daniel 7:[123]

> And there I saw One, who had a head of days,/ And His head was white like wool,/ And with Him was another being whose countenance had the appearance of a man,/ And his face was full of graciousness, like one of the holy angels. And I asked the angel who went with me and showed me all the hidden things, concerning that Son of Man, who he

---

[119] Darrell D. Hannah, "The Elect Son of Man of the *Parables of Enoch*," in *'Who is This Son of Man?': The Latest Scholarship on a Puzzling Expression of the Historical Jesus*, ed. Larry W. Hurtado and Paul L. Owen et al. (New York: Bloomsbury T & T Clark, 2011), 134.
[120] Ibid., 132-133.
[121] Ibid., 137.
[122] Ibid., 142.
[123] Ibid., 143.

was, and whence he was, (and) why he went with the Head of Days? And he answered and said unto me: This is the Son of Man who hath righteousness, with Whom dwelleth righteousness.[124]

Scholars debate whether the appellation is used as a title when for instance in 46:2 the Enochic figure is called "the Son of Man."[125] Whether a title or not, "the Son of Man" refers back both to the one "whose countenance had the appearance of a man" in 46:1,[126] a passage which is itself alluding to the "son of man" of Daniel 7:13.[127] In *Similitudes*, in 48:10 and 52:4, the Enochic "Son of Man" is identified with the Messiah,[128] being called "Anointed"[129] (the phrase for "Messiah" in Hebrew is literally translated as "Anointed (One)").[130] The eschatological figure has the role of a judge, and the text frequently states that he sits on God's very own throne, the "throne of glory."[131] The figure thus sits on God's throne and acts as eschatological judge, suggesting that

---

[124] R.H. Charles, trans., *The Book of Enoch the Prophet* (California/Massachusetts: Weiser Books, 2012 ed.), 822-830 of 2,415, Kindle edition.
[125] Vermes, *Jesus the Jew*, 175.
[126] Charles, trans., *The Book of Enoch the Prophet*, 822 of 2,415.
[127] Collins, *The Scepter and the Star*, 197.
[128] Casey, *The Solution to the 'Son of Man' Problem*, 1,505 of 6,420; Collins, *The Scepter and the Star*, 203; Kee, "Christology in Mark's Gospel," 191.
[129] Charles, trans., *The Book of Enoch the Prophet*, 904 and 951 of 2,415.
[130] Boyarin, *The Jewish* Gospels, 26; Horbury, *Jewish Messianism and the Cult of Christ*, 7.
[131] Collins, *The Scepter and the Star*, 162; Hannah, "The Elect Son of Man of the *Parables of Enoch*," 130, 145.

he is divine to a certain extent, or at least highly exalted.[132] The text also indicates that the figure is pre-existent, with four passages affirming "both an ontological and pre-mundane pre-existence."[133] The Enochic "son of man" is even worshiped in 48:5, further indicating that the figure is divine.[134]

4. 4 Ezra

4 Ezra, another apocalyptic text from the 1st century CE, also uses Daniel 7 as a basis for the portrait of a figure that the text identifies as the Messiah.[135] *Similitudes* and *4 Ezra* were probably written independently of each other, as one text never references the other, and their similarities are best explained as a common reliance on the book of Daniel.[136] But whether they were written independently from the Gospels is debatable. For instance, the phrase "throne of glory" occurs both in *Similitudes* and in the King James Bible version of Matthew 25:31,[137] indicating that *Similitudes* was drawing from the Gospel, that Jesus (or the evangelist) was deliberately drawing from *Similitudes*, or that "throne of glory" was simply

---

[132] Collins and Collins, *King and Messiah as Son of God*, 94.
[133] Hannah, "The Elect Son of Man of the *Parables of Enoch*," 151.
[134] Ibid., 148; Collins, *The Scepter and the Star*, 204.
[135] Boyarin, *The Jewish Gospels*, 95.
[136] Collins and Collins, *King and Messiah as Son of God*, 98.
[137] In Charles's translation, "throne of glory" occurs 3 times in *Similitudes* (*The Book of Enoch the Prophet*, 815; 1,001, and 1,115 of 2,415). In the ESV, the phrase "glorious throne" is stated in Matthew 25:31, but the King James Bible more literally translates the Greek phrase. Given how construct-absolute relationships are formed in the Semitic languages of Hebrew and Aramaic, the Greek would also constitute a literal translation of the expression that Jesus most probably used in Aramaic. Also, according to Casey, *Similitudes* was originally in Aramaic, therefore the phrase of "throne of glory" used in *Similitudes* may have been identical to the one Jesus used in 25:31 of the book of Matthew.

a common way of referring to God's throne. It seems certain though that both *Similitudes* and *4 Ezra* are of Jewish origin, with Collins arguing that it is highly unlikely that a "Son of Man" individual would be included in a Christian text, if it was never apparent that the "Son of Man" was Jesus.[138] The Jewish apocalyptic texts would thus represent two non-Christian examples of the Danielic "son of man" being implicitly interpreted not only as an individual, but also as the Messiah.

4 Ezra was probably written originally in Hebrew or Aramaic (though not extant in those languages today).[139] "It is clear that the imagery and eschatological expectation conveyed in 13.1-13 is drawn out of Daniel 7, and applied to a specific Messianic figure (13.21-56)."[140] Although the phrase "son of man" itself is not used in *4 Ezra*, the text evidently incorporates the imagery of Daniel 7, and even specifically 7:13, into the portrait of its salvific figure.[141] For instance, 13:2-3 is clearly using the imagery of Daniel 7:13:[142]

> And behold, a great wind arose from the sea
> so that it stirred up all its waves. And I
> looked, and behold, this wind made
> something like the figure of a man come up
> out of the heart of the sea. And I looked, and

---

[138] Collins and Collins, *King and Messiah as Son of God*, 87. See Collins, *The Scepter and the Star*, 196; Hannah, "The Elect Son of Man of the *Parables of Enoch*," 135.

[139] Michael E. Stone and Matthias Henze, *4 Ezra and 2 Baruch: Translations, Introductions, and Notes* (Minneapolis, Minnesota: Fortress Press, 2013), 112 of 2,532, Kindle edition.

[140] Owen, "Problems with Casey's 'Solution'," 47.

[141] Collins and Collins, *King and Messiah as Son of God*, 95.

[142] Ibid.; Collins, *The Scepter and the Star*, 205.

behold, that man flew with the clouds of heaven; and wherever he turned his face to look, everything under his gaze trembled.[143]

The man is explicitly referred to as "Messiah" in 7:28 and 7:29.[144] The man rising up from the ocean's Messianic status is confirmed, for he is later described in 13:26 as "he whom the Most High has been keeping for many ages, through whom he will deliver his creation."[145] One can thus infer that the Danielic "son of man" was not only interpreted as an individual, but also as a Messianic figure, for Daniel 7:13 was incorporated by *Ezra* into the portrait of its expected Messianic figure.[146]

5. Rabbinic Literature

The first known interpretation in rabbinic writings was by R. Akiba (40 CE to c. 135 CE), whose teachings are often quoted in the *Mishnah*.[147] In *Sanhedrin* 38b of the Babylonian Talmud, R. Akiba indirectly interpreted the Danielic "son of man" as the Messiah by his understanding of

---

[143] Stone and Henze, trans., *4 Ezra and 2 Baruch: Translations, Introductions, and Notes*, 1,258 of 2,532.
[144] Michael E. Stone, "The Messiah in 4 Ezra," *Judaisms and Their Messiahs at the Turn of the Christian Era*, ed. Jacob Neusner et al. (New York: Cambridge University Press, 1987), 210.
[145] Stone and Henze, trans., *4 Ezra and 2 Baruch: Translations, Introductions, and Notes*, 1,292 of 2,532.
[146] Owen, "Problems with Casey's 'Solution'," 47.
[147] Vermes, *Jesus the Jew*, 171; *Encyclopædia Britannica*, "Akiba ben Joseph (Jewish sage and rabbinic founder)," last accessed April 23, 2019, http://www.britannica.com/EBchecked/topic/11606/Akiba-ben-Joseph.

the plural "thrones" from Daniel's vision in 7:9.[148] He inferred that there were two thrones, one belonging to God ("the Ancient of Days") and the other belonging to David.[149] He thus probably understood that the "son of man" in Daniel 7:13 was the expected Davidic Messiah.[150]

6. Son of Man Concept?

On the whole, there was arguably a "spectrum of Messianic expectation" in Second Temple Judaism.[151] Collins observed that there were "four basic Messianic paradigms" of "king, priest, prophet, and heavenly messiah," with the "kingly" paradigm being the most common (though not necessarily derived from the Danielic passage).[152] Collins wrote that the "'heavenly messiah' paradigm is somewhat different from the others, since it is not defined by function, and can overlap with the other paradigms."[153]

What can be inferred from the evidence of the ancient texts close to the time of Jesus, especially those dating approximately from the 1st century CE, is that many common assumptions were held regarding the figure from Daniel 7:13. First, the two texts of *Similitudes* and *4 Ezra* take the figure in Daniel 7:13 not only to be an individual, but also to be the Messiah.[154] Second, the two 1st century CE apocalyptic texts

---

[148] Vermes, *Jesus the Jew*, 171; Rabbi Hersh Goldwurm, general ed., *The ArtScroll Series/ Schottenstein Daf Yomi Edition Talmud Bavli/ Tractate Sanhedrin Vol. 1* (New York: Mesorah Publications, Ltd., 2002 ed.), 38b.
[149] Ibid.; Bowman and Komoszewski, *Putting Jesus in His Place*, 2,795 of 4,522; See Boyarin, *The Jewish Gospels*, 40-41.
[150] Dalman, *Words of Jesus*, 245.
[151] Collins, *The Scepter and the Star*, 214.
[152] Ibid., 18.
[153] Ibid.
[154] Ibid., 188, 211.

and the two Qumranic texts use Daniel in depicting a highly exalted figure, possibly of even divine status.

However, saying that common assumptions about the Danielic "son of man" were held in texts around the time of Jesus is not tantamount to saying that there was a universal concept regarding the Messiah derived from the Danielic passage. It may even be argued that the figures depicted in the texts all correspond to the "heavenly messiah" paradigm, but there was nonetheless probably no fixed or unified Son of Man concept.[155] The Enochic "son of man" acts only as a heavenly judge at the end of days, whereas the Messianic figure from *Ezra* comes out from the ocean and has an earthly role in restoring Israel (not as a part of the final Judgment).[156] The Son of Man was perhaps not even a title at the time, or at least not a common one as Messiah was. Yet for each of the examples presented Daniel was "the point of departure for the imagery" in painting either the portrait of a Messianic figure or a highly exalted eschatological figure.[157] Consequently, there may not have been a fixed concept of the Son of Man, but ideas regarding the Danielic figure that were "in the air" at the time of Jesus implied that the Danielic "son of man" was interpreted as an individual and as a highly exalted eschatological figure (if not a Messianic one).[158]

C. "The Son of Man" in the New Testament: The Question of Authenticity

---

[155] Burkett, *The Son of Man Debate*, 120; Long, *L'Invention du Christianisme*, 118.
[156] Collins, *The Scepter and the Star*, 213; Stone, "The Messiah in 4 Ezra," 212.
[157] Bock, "The Use of Daniel 7 in Jesus' Trial," 85, 86, 90.
[158] Witherington, *The Christology of Jesus*, 252.

Before examining the use of the expression in the Gospel of Mark, it is important to consider whether the designation and the allusions to Daniel truly came from Jesus. In critically examining the New Testament, historians have used various criteria in order to ascertain whether or not a saying is authentic. Over the past few centuries, numerous criteria have been applied to the Gospels in order to determine which sayings from Jesus could be considered genuine and which ones were creations or alterations from the early church. Three of the most common ones that are applicable are the criteria of dissimilarity, multiple attestation, and general coherence.[159] According to Craig Evans, dissimilarity "requires sayings and deeds attributed to Jesus to be dissimilar to (or inconsistent with) the theology of the early church" or to "tendencies and emphases within the Judaism of Jesus' day."[160] Multiple attestation "refers to sayings and actions attributed to Jesus that appear in two or more independent sources," which suggest that they "were not invented by a single writer."[161] The criterion of coherence requires that material be consistent "with material judged authentic on the basis of the other criteria."[162] If one applies these to the phrase "the Son of Man" and the Danielic allusions, the criteria show that they most likely originated from the Rabbi himself. However, as Darrell Bock notes, "these criteria serve better as a supplemental argument for authenticity than as criteria that can establish authenticity."[163]

---

[159] Evans, *Fabricating Jesus*, 48-51.
[160] Ibid., 50.
[161] Ibid., 48.
[162] Ibid., 51.
[163] Darrell L. Bock, *Studying the Historical Jesus: A Guide to Sources and Methods* (Michigan: Baker Academic, 2002), 4,037 of 4,412, Kindle edition;

1. Double-Dissimilarity

The first criterion I will apply is that of *double dissimilarity*: "Texts have a solid claim to authenticity if they are similar to but distinct from Judaism in some respects and if they are similar to the early church in some respects but also distinct at other points."[164] In order to adequately apply this criterion, it seems necessary to first display the following table, which presents the number of times "the Son of Man" is quoted in the books of the New Testament outside of the Gospels, and the books from the Bible that are quoted in each New Testament book:[165]

Cf. Bowman and Komoszewski, *Putting Jesus in His Place*, 4,138 of 4,522. William Lane Craig states sates that the criteria of authenticity "can only be properly used positively, to demonstrate authenticity. In other words, the criteria state sufficient, not necessary, conditions of historicity" (William Lane Craig, *Reasonable Faith: Christian Truth and Apologetics* (Illinois: Crossway, 2008), 292).

[164] Bock, *Studying the Historical Jesus*, 4,027 of 4,412; Cf. N.T. Wright, *Jesus and the Victory of God: Christian Origins and the Question of God, Volume 2* (London, UK: Fortress Press, 1996), 2,868 of 43,468, Kindle edition.

[165] Data in table gathered using *The Holy Bible, New International Version* (Michigan: Zondervan, 2011), and using *Accordance*.

New Testament Book	Number of times "the Son of Man" occurs	Number of quotations from Daniel	Bible books quoted (number of different chapters quoted from book)
Acts	1 (**7:56**)	0	Genesis (4), Exodus (5), Deuteronomy (1), Psalms (6), Isaiah (4), Joel (1), Amos (2), and Habakkuk (1)
Romans	0	0	Genesis (5), Exodus (3), Leviticus (2), Deuteronomy (4), 2 Samuel (1), 1 Kings (1), Job (1), Psalms (14), Proverbs (2), Ecclesiastes (1), Isaiah (13), Jeremiah (1), Ezekiel (1), Hosea (2), Joel (1), Habakkuk (1), and Malachi (1)
1 Corinthians	0	0	Genesis (1), Exodus (1), Deuteronomy (1), Job (1), Psalms (3), Isaiah (6), Jeremiah (1), and Hosea (1)

New Testament Book	Number of times "the Son of Man" occurs	Number of quotations from Daniel	Bible books quoted (number of different chapters quoted from book)
2 Corinthians	0	0	Genesis (1), Exodus (1), Leviticus (1), Deuteronomy (1), 2 Samuel (1), Psalms (2), Isaiah (2), Jeremiah (2), and Ezekiel (2)
Galatians	0	0	Genesis (7), Leviticus (2), Deuteronomy (2), Isaiah (1), and Habakkuk (1)
Ephesians	0	0	Genesis (1), Deuteronomy (1), and Psalms (2)
Philippians	0	0	Deuteronomy (1)
Colossians	0	0	None
1 Thessalonians	0	0	None
2 Thessalonians	0	0	None
1 Timothy	0	0	Deuteronomy (1) and Luke 10:7
2 Timothy	0	0	None
Titus	0	0	None
Philemon	0	0	None

New Testament Book	Number of times "the Son of Man" occurs	Number of quotations from Daniel	Bible books quoted (number of different chapters quoted from book)
Hebrews	0	0	Genesis (4), Exodus (3), Deuteronomy (4), Numbers (1), 2 Samuel (1), 1 Chronicles (1), Psalms (11), Proverbs (2), Isaiah (2), Jeremiah (1), Habakkuk (1), and Haggai (1)
James	0	0	Genesis (1), Exodus (1), Leviticus (1), Deuteronomy (1), and Proverbs (1)
1 Peter	0	0	Leviticus (2), Isaiah (4), Psalms (2), and Proverbs (2)
2 Peter	0	0	Proverbs (1) and Mark 9:7
1 John	0	0	None
2 John	0	0	None
3 John	0	0	None
Jude	0	0	None from the Bible
Revelation	0	4 (3 from Daniel 7:13)	Deuteronomy (1), Psalms (4), Isaiah (6), Jeremiah (3), Ezekiel (1), Daniel (1), Hosea (1), and Zechariah (2)
Summary	1	4	Daniel only quoted in book of Revelation

None of the Epistles either uses the designation Son of Man or quotes Daniel, yet the book of Revelation does quote Daniel 7:13 on three occasions. Without the definite article, the phrase "son of man" also occurs in Revelation 1:13 and 14:14 in passages alluding to Daniel 7:13. The Epistles were written approximately between the dates of 49 CE and 90 CE, while the book of Revelation, widely considered to have been the last New Testament book written, dates from around 95 CE.[166] Some scholars have theorized that the designation was created on the basis of Daniel 7:13, but that it was added sometime after the Epistles were written.[167] Was the designation then added on the basis of the Danielic allusion in Revelation?[168] It seems unlikely, one reason being that the consensus among scholars is that the Synoptic Gospels were already written by then, with the Gospel of Mark, in particular, having been written several decades beforehand.[169] Second, if it were introduced that late, it would be difficult to explain why the debate over its meaning had already begun around 108 CE with the bishop

---

[166] *NLT Parallel Study Bible*, 2,107- 2,409.
[167] James H. Charlesworth in Marcus J. Borg, *Images of Jesus Today*, (Valley Forge, Pennsylvania.: Trinity Press International, 1994), 46; Müller, *The Expression 'Son of Man' and the Development of Christology*, 166-167.
[168] Cf. Müller, *The Expression 'Son of Man' and the Development of Christology*, 167-168.
[169] The Letter of 1 Timothy, attributed to Paul (though disputed), which was written around 64 CE, already quotes Luke 10:7. At least part of Luke was then already probably written by then, a Gospel which is thought to be dependent on Mark. Also, 2 Peter, attributed to Peter (though also disputed) and written around 67 CE, quotes Mark 9:7 (*NLT Parallel Study Bible*, 2,283- 2,383).

Ignatius of Antioch.[170] Although Ignatius studied under the Apostle John,[171] who is traditionally regarded as the author of the book of Revelation, the bishop did not even interpret the phrase as a title derived from Daniel 7:13, but as simply denoting Jesus' humanity.[172] In fact, apart from the book of Revelation, which was written *after* the Gospels, only Jesus ever references the book of Daniel at all in the New Testament:[173]

---

[170] Burkett, *The Son of Man Debate*, 7; Müller, *The Expression 'Son of Man' and the Development of Christology*, 12.
[171] David Bentley Hart, *The Story of Christianity*, (New York: Metro Books, 2007), 31.
[172] Burkett, *The Son of Man Debate*, 7.
[173] Data in table gathered *The Holy Bible, New International Version* and using *Accordance*. The phrase "with the clouds of heaven" in Mark 14:62 can be considered a quotation of Daniel 7:13, given that Daniel 7:13 is the only verse of the *Tanakh* with the phrase "with the clouds of heaven" (*Accordance*). I am assuming that when Jesus says "on the clouds of heaven" in Matthew 24:30 and 26:64, he is quoting Daniel 7:13's "with the clouds of heaven." Despite not being a perfect quotation, it is nevertheless reasonable to call it a "quotation," especially since the Aramaic behind the Greek words could have indeed been identical to the ones in Daniel 7:13.

Gospel	Number of times "the Son of Man" is uttered by Jesus	Number of quotations from Daniel	Danielic quotations put on Jesus' lips
Matthew	30	2	2
Mark	14[174]	1	1
Luke	24	0	0
John	11	0	0
Summary	**79**[175]	**3**	**3**

As one can observe from the two tables, there is a stark contrast in the use of "the Son of Man" compared to the rest of the New Testament. Seventy-nine out of the eighty-two Gospel occurrences of the term "Son of Man" are spoken by Jesus, and all the references in the Gospels to the book of Daniel are put on Jesus' lips alone. Although there may be only few explicit quotations from Daniel, only Jesus made them. There are also 19 further occurrences in which Jesus is probably alluding to Daniel 7:13 by combining "the Son of Man" with a conjugated form of the verb "to come," which is a pairing that is also only made by Jesus in the New Testament.[176] Daniel 7:13 is thus directly or indirectly alluded

---

[174] The number includes the two additional occurrences in indirect speech.
[175] Although John 5:27 has the definite article in the ESV, "Son of Man" does not have the definite article in the underlying Greek, therefore there are 78 occurrences of "the Son of Man" in the original Greek.
[176] *Accordance*; Vermes, *Jesus the Jew*, 178. In the ESV of the *Tanakh*, Ezekiel 21:14 and Daniel 7:13 are the only verses which feature a "son of man" as the subject of a form of the verb "to come" (*Accordance*). In Ezekiel 21:14, God tells Ezekiel to "let the sword come down." In this verse, the conjugated form of the verb "to come" follows the verb "to let," so the "son of man" in this verse—in this case the prophet Ezekiel—is not directly performing the action of coming. However, the "son of man" in Daniel 7:13 and the "Son of Man" in Jesus' sayings *are* directly performing

to in about 28% of the occasions in which Jesus utters "Son of Man" in the four Gospels.[177] Thus both the use of "the Son of Man" *and* the use of the book of Daniel seem to have been distinctive of Jesus. Jesus' use of the book of Daniel and of the expression "the Son of Man" was thus dissimilar from that of the early church. Also, the book and the expression are both rooted in Judaism, but Jesus' use of them is unique: with the definite article, he used an expression that was virtually unheard of before his coming, and the Son of Man sayings evidently alluding to Daniel find no exact equivalent in either 1st century CE apocalyptic texts or the two Qumran texts. Therefore, Jesus' use of Daniel and of "the Son of Man" meets the criterion of double-dissimilarity.

2. Multiple Attestation

Furthermore, the Son of Man sayings originated indisputably early, and are multiply attested in many independent and early sources, including Mark, John, Q,[178] and the "Gospel of the Hebrews."[179] The theoretical document known as Q mainly consists of sayings of Jesus, at least some of which are believed to go back to traditions which even pre-date Mark.[180] Consequently, the designation

---

the action of coming. By combining "Son of Man" and a form of the verb "to come," Jesus was thus most probably deliberately alluding to Daniel 7:13 among all the verses of the *Tanakh*.

[177] Later it will be shown how actually more than 28% of the sayings probably allude to Daniel 7:13, though in more subtle ways.

[178] Q is the content that is found both in Matthew and Luke, but that is not also included in Mark.

[179] Crossan, *The Historical Jesus*, 6,013 of 12,350. The "Gospel of the Hebrews" is a possibly independent though non-canonical account which, according to Evans, scholars generally consider to have been written around 140 CE (Evans, *Fabricating Jesus*, 61).

[180] Bock, *Studying the Historical Jesus*, 3,380 of 4,412.

of Son of Man and the allusions to Daniel, which are not used by the early church, are included in what are considered the two earliest independent sources: Mark and Q.

3. Coherence

Not only is the designation *dissimilar* to the use of the early church and multiply attested by different independent sources, but it is also *coherent* with Jesus' teachings and character.[181] Jesus often taught in parables and figures of speech, and though he revealed spiritual truths in his parables, he also simultaneously concealed them by the fact that they were communicated in the form of stories.[182] Ambiguity and subtlety was characteristic of Jesus, to the point that even his own disciples needed an explanation at times, such as in the pericope in Mark 7:1-23. In the same way, the expression "the Son of Man" has an inherent ambiguity that may have been used by Jesus to reveal in veiled form something about his identity.[183] In addition, Witherington puts forth that "only in Daniel 7 do we find the two major *leitmotifs* of the sayings material in the Gospels that scholars generally agree go back to Jesus: the reference to" the "son of man" and to the kingdom of God.[184] The fact that the two *leitmotifs* that are

---

[181] Bock, *Studying the Historical Jesus*, 4,034 of 4,412.

[182] Ben Witherington, III, *The Gospel of Mark: A Socio-Rhetorical Commentary* (Michigan and Cambridge, UK: Wm. B. Eerdmans Publishing Company, 2001), 735 of 7,980, Kindle edition.

[183] D. A. Carson, "Matthew," in *The Expositor's Bible Commentary*, Volume 8, ed. Frank E. Gaebelein (Michigan: Zondervan Pub. House, 1984), 212; Crossan, *The Historical Jesus*, 5,709 of 12,350; Harry L. Chronis, "To Reveal and to Conceal: A Literary-Critical Perspective on 'the Son of Man' in Mark," *New Testament Studies* 51, no. 4 (October 1, 2005): 478, last accessed November 3, 2013, ATLA Religion Database with ATLASerials, EBSCOhost; Witherington, *The Gospel of Mark*, 735 of 7,980.

[184] Witherington, *The Christology of Jesus*, 242.

prevalent in Jesus' sayings occur solely in Daniel 7 further corroborates the point that the allusions to Daniel genuinely came from Jesus.

4. Criterion of Embarrassment

Even the criterion of embarrassment is applicable in two Son of Man sayings, if only indirectly. The criterion, which is arguably one of the strongest ones in assessing authenticity, refers to "embarrassing" sayings or deeds that would make someone look less than perfect.[185] Towards the end of the Olivet Discourse of Mark 13, Jesus tells his disciples, "But concerning that day or that hour, no one knows, not even the angels in heaven, nor the Son, but only the Father."[186] The verse is evidently problematic, given that Jesus is affirming that he does not know when his predictions would take place. It is therefore highly unlikely that the early church would invent such a saying: "its offence seals its genuineness."[187] Yet the problematic saying, which is probably authentic, is precisely referring to the predictions made beforehand which included "the Son of Man coming in clouds."[188] If Jesus' saying about not knowing when predicted events would occur is authentic, then he must have made some predictions in the first place.

Moreover, after Jesus' first Passion prediction, Jesus, in response to Peter's reaction, calls him "Satan" in Mark 8:33. Again, it is highly unlikely that the early church would invent a saying of Jesus' in which the Apostle Peter is called

---

[185] Erik Larson (class notes).
[186] Mark 13:32.
[187] Vincent Taylor, *The Gospel According to St. Mark*, (London, UK: Macmillan & Co. Ltd., 1959), 522.
[188] Mark 13:26.

"Satan."[189] Peter had reacted to the Passion prediction by telling Jesus the following (a saying recorded in Matthew): "Far be it from you, Lord! This shall never happen to you."[190] Jesus follows his response to Peter with the admonishment that following him required sacrifice: "For whoever would save his life will lose it, but whoever loses his life for my sake and the gospel's will save it."[191] Jesus' rebuke of Peter in Mark 8:33 and his admonishment that every disciple should "take up his cross"[192], when taken together, imply that Jesus must have at least made an allusion to his own forthcoming sufferings. The prediction of his looming suffering and death is precisely in the Son of Man saying of Mark 8:31 (in indirect speech).

As a result, both the designation and the references to Daniel most probably came from Jesus of Nazareth. Joachim Jeremias affirmed that the designation of Son of Man was therefore "rooted in the tradition of the sayings of Jesus right from the beginning; as a result, it was sacrosanct, and no-one dared to eliminate it."[193]

D. Jesus Was Referring Exclusively to the "Son of Man" from Daniel 7:13

Outside of the New Testament, the definite designation occurs only in *Similitudes* in the first century CE, which is clearly alluding to Daniel 7:13. The demonstrative is usually employed, but the definite article is used at least once in 46:2. In addition, *Similitudes* has "an initial quotation of the

---

[189] Joachim Jeremias, *New Testament Theology* (New York: Charles Scribner's Sons, 1971), 283;
[190] Matthew 16:22.
[191] Mark 8:35.
[192] Mark 8:34.
[193] Jeremias, *New Testament Theology*, 266.

Danielic phrase, without the article," and "is followed by frequent references back to it, in phrases which are all, in one way or another, in a definite form."[194] Moule contended that Jesus, in analogous fashion, was also using the definite state to the previously mentioned figure in Daniel 7:13, which would provide an explanation as to why he *continually* used the definite article.[195]

Everything (or almost everything) "that Jesus taught—from the rule of God to the Golden Rule—is rooted in Scripture."[196] It is therefore significant that the Aramaic *bar enash* ("son of man") is mentioned solely in Daniel 7:13.[197] Occam's razor can thus be applied in this case: Jesus' continual use of the definite "*the* Son of Man" was anaphoric; Jesus was simply referring to the indefinite "son of man" in Daniel 7:13, rather than using an idiomatic expression.[198]

In total, there are five reasons for which one may assume that Jesus was referring specifically and solely to the "son of man" in Daniel 7:13 (not only in Mark, but in all the Gospels): (1) because Jesus used the definite article *consistently*, he was probably referring to a specific "son of man";[199] (2) given that unlike *Similitudes*, only Daniel indisputably pre-

---

[194] C.F.D. Moule, *The Origin of Christology* (Cambridge, UK: Cambridge University Press, 1977), 15.
[195] Ibid., 16.
[196] Evans, *Fabricating Jesus*, 38-39.
[197] Dalman, *Words of Jesus*, 256; Metzger Müller et al., *The Oxford Companion to the Bible* (New York: Oxford University Press, 1993), 712 (1993).
[198] Adela Yarbro Collins, "The Origin of the Designation of Jesus as 'Son of Man,'" *Harvard Theological Review* 80, no. 4 (October 1, 1987): 404, last accessed January 22, 2014, ATLA Religion Database with ATLASerials, EBSCOhost; Owen and Shepherd, "Speaking Up for Qumran, Dalman and the Son of Man," 112.
[199] Evans, *Fabricating Jesus*, 149.

dates the time of Jesus,[200] and that Jesus' teachings were grounded in the Hebrew Bible, it is more likely that Daniel—rather than *Similitudes*—was his source for the expression; (3) the only verse Jesus ever explicitly quotes from the *Tanakh* that includes the phrase "son of man" is Daniel 7:13; (4) Jesus had only one "son of man" to quote from in Aramaic in the *Tanakh*: the one in Daniel 7:13; (5) the use of "Son of Man" and the allusions to Daniel are distinctive of Jesus in the New Testament, and only Daniel 7 contains the two important *leitmotifs*—kingdom of God and the Son of Man—that are found in Jesus' teachings, therefore it is probable that the allusions to Daniel genuinely came from Jesus himself.[201] The exegesis of Mark in the next chapter will examine how Jesus interpreted the figure and then how he saw himself as the fulfillment of Daniel's vision in 7:13-14.[202]

---

[200] Richard N. Longenecker, "'Son of Man' as a Self-Designation of Jesus," *Journal Of The Evangelical Theological Society* 12, no. 3 (June 1, 1969): 153, last accessed January 22, 2014, ATLA Religion Database with ATLASerials, EBSCOhost.
[201] Witherington, *The Christology of Jesus*, 242.
[202] Longenecker, "'Son of Man' as a Self-Designation of Jesus," 158.

III. EXEGESIS OF MARK

Mark is the shortest of the four canonical Gospels, containing 661 verses.[1] It is now the general consensus among scholars that Mark was the first Gospel to be written. It was written most probably between 60 and 70 CE, or a few years immediately following 70 CE.[2] The Son of Man sayings in Mark are roughly organized in the following way: those relating to Jesus' earthly ministry are towards the beginning of the Gospel, those of his suffering and death towards the middle, and those relating to his future exaltation and return at the end of Mark.[3] The first question that must be answered is whether Jesus was referring exclusively to himself. From that, one could then assess whether Jesus used the Son of Man as a Messianic title or not.

A. The Son of Man Sayings in Mark

Mark 2:10: "But that you may know that the Son of Man has authority on earth to forgive sins."

In the Gospel of Mark, in response to faith, Jesus first tells the paralytic that his sins are forgiven, before proving it by healing him. Jesus here makes a connection between sin and sickness.[4] However, as Jesus himself makes known in

---

[1] Darrell L. Bock, *Studying the Historical Jesus: A Guide to Sources and Methods* (Michigan: Baker Academic, 2002), 3,370 of 4,412, Kindle edition.

[2] John Drane, *Introducing the New Testament: Third Edition* (Minneapolis, Minnesota: Fortress Press, 2011), 189.

[3] Harry L. Chronis, "To Reveal and to Conceal: A Literary-Critical Perspective on 'the Son of Man' in Mark," *New Testament Studies* 51, no. 4 (October 1, 2005): 479, last accessed November 3, 2013, ATLA Religion Database with ATLASerials, EBSCOhost.

[4] Barnabas Lindars, *Jesus Son of Man: A Fresh Examination of the Son of Man Sayings in the Gospels in the Light of Recent Research* (Michigan: Wm. B. Eerdmans, 1983), 45; Martina E. Martin, "It's My Prerogative: Jesus'

John 9:2-3, he did not consider that *all* diseases were caused by a person's sins. Jesus is unmistakably referring to himself and not another individual, but some scholars have postulated that in 2:10, Jesus was making a generic statement in which Jesus was including himself. The main question would therefore be whether Jesus made a statement that was only true for himself or a generic statement in which he included himself.[5]

As Mark 2:7 implies, forgiving of sins was God's exclusive right, not something that could be ascribed to just any person.[6] When Jesus forgave the paralytic's sins, the religious leaders who were present thought to themselves, "Why does this man speak like that? He is blaspheming! Who can forgive sins but God alone?"[7] Jesus was either being accused of claiming to be God or of claiming to exercise God's prerogative.[8] Although the *Tanakh* never explicitly affirms that forgiveness of sins is God's prerogative, it may be inferred from passages such as Exodus 34:6-7, Psalm 51:4, Psalm 103:3, Isaiah 43:25, 44:22, 55:7, Jeremiah 50:20, Daniel

---

Authority to Grant Forgiveness and Healing on Earth," *Journal Of Religious Thought* 59, (January 1, 2007): 71, last accessed January 18, 2014, ATLA Religion Database with ATLASerials, EBSCOhost.

[5] Witherington, *The Christology of Jesus*, 249.

[6] Lewis Scott Hay, "Son of Man in Mark 2:10 and 2:28," *Journal of Biblical Literature* 89, no. 1 (March 1, 1970): 72, last accessed January 10, 2014, ATLA Religion Database with ATLASerials, EBSCOhost; Martin, "It's My Prerogative," 72; C.F.D. Moule, *The Origin of Christology* (Cambridge, UK: Cambridge University Press, 1977), 14.

[7] Mark 2:7.

[8] *NLT Parallel Study Bible* (Illinois: Tyndale House Publishers, Inc., 2011), 1,903.

9:9, and Micah 7:18.[9] For example, Daniel 9:9 states the following: "To the Lord our God belong mercy and forgiveness, for we have rebelled against him." It is also reasonable to assume, as Daniel Johansson argues, that "only the one who has been sinned against can forgive."[10] And that forgiveness would belong to God alone, because ultimately it is against God any and every sin is committed.[11] A priest could perhaps *declare* that someone's sins were forgiven (e.g., at Yom Kippur), and a prophet could sometimes also declare forgiveness (e.g., 2 Samuel 12:13) or mediate for others, but only God could actually forgive people.[12] From the *Tanakh*, one could argue at most that perhaps the priests at the Temple could forgive sins when they received sin offerings from the people (e.g., Leviticus 4:31).[13] Yet it seems to have

---

[9] Robert M. Bowman Jr. and J. Ed Komoszewski, *Putting Jesus in His Place: The Case for the Deity of Christ* (Michigan: Kregel Publications, 2007), 2,368 of 4,522, Kindle edition; Robert Jamieson et al., "Commentary Critical and Explanatory on the Whole Bible," *Christian Classics Ethereal Library*, last accessed April 26, 2019, http://www.ccel.org/ccel/jamieson/jfb.txt, 1871; Daniel Johansson, "'Who Can Forgive Sins but God Alone?' Human and Angelic Agents, and Divine Forgiveness in Early Judaism," *Journal for the Study of the New Testament* 33, no. 4 (June 1, 2011): 352, last accessed January 18, 2014, ATLA Religion Database with ATLASerials, EBSCOhost; *NLT Parallel Study Bible*, 1,758.
[10] Johansson, "Who Can Forgive Sins but God Alone?" 352-353.
[11] See for instance Genesis 39:9 Psalm 51:4.
[12] Johansson, "Who Can Forgive Sins but God Alone?" 369; *NLT Parallel Study Bible*, 1,827; Ben Witherington, III, *The Gospel of Mark: A Socio-Rhetorical Commentary* (Michigan and Cambridge, UK: Wm. B. Eerdmans Publishing Company, 2001), 1,727 of 7,980, Kindle edition.
[13] James D. G. Dunn, *The Parting of Ways: Between Christianity and Judaism and Their Significance for the Character of Christianity* (London, UK: SCM Press, 1991), 45.

been unprecedented in Judaism for *anyone* besides God to have directly forgiven anyone's sins on their own authority.[14]

The only possible exceptions of a human forgiving may come from Qumran, in the texts of *Prayer of Nabonidus* and the *Damascus Document*.[15] However in both cases it is unclear grammatically whether God or the person in question is doing the forgiving.[16] If it were the person doing the forgiving in each case, the texts give no indication whether they were merely relaying a message from God or if they actually had the authority to forgive sins (granted to them by God).[17] What seems clear, however, is that Jesus was not making a generic statement, not even one referring more specifically to prophets or Jewish healers and exorcists, given that no evidence conclusively indicates that they could ever do anything further than declare or mediate forgiveness of sins.[18] That Jesus' authority was unprecedented is confirmed by the reaction of the crowds watching, who exclaim in Mark 2:12, "We never saw anything like this!"[19] Consequently, the evidence indicates that the saying was most probably referring exclusively to Jesus, and that Jesus was therefore not making a generic statement.

It may seem superfluous at first glance for Jesus to say that his authority in forgiving is "on earth." Why would he specify "on earth"? It is possible Jesus said it merely in an idiomatic manner (tantamount to "throughout the earth"), but on the basis of Jesus' use of "on earth" throughout the

---

[14] Dunn, *The Parting of Ways*, 46.
[15] Johansson, "Who Can Forgive Sins but God Alone?" 356-357, 365.
[16] Ibid., 356-357.
[17] Ibid., 358.
[18] Ibid., 366.
[19] Geza Vermes, *Jesus the Jew* (Pennsylvania: Fortress Press, 1973), 180.

Gospels, one observes that he often states "on earth" in order to contrast with "in heaven."[20] Excluding the current verse of Mark 2:10 (and the two other parallel verses), Jesus says "on earth" 14 times in the Gospels.[21] In 9 of the occurrences (or nearly 2/3 of them), Jesus says "on earth" as opposed to heaven (the other ones tend to have the meaning of "in all the earth"). If he was also saying it as opposed (or in addition) to heaven, Jesus' comment "on earth" becomes clear if he was referring to the Danielic figure.[22] The "son of man" in Daniel receives authority in "the clouds of heaven," but Jesus affirmed in 2:10 that he also had the same authority "on earth" (in this case specifically to forgive sins).[23] This view is supported by Jesus' post-resurrection statement in Matthew 28:18: "All authority in heaven and on earth has been given to me." His utterance of "on earth" is thus more understandable if Jesus had the Danielic figure in mind.[24] If Jesus was using merely a circumlocutionary expression to refer to himself, it would have been redundant to indicate "on earth," whereas it is *not* obvious that the Danielic character

---

[20] Bowman and Komoszewski, *Putting Jesus in His Place*, 2,368 of 4,522.
[21] *Accordance*. With the exception of Matthew 6:10, in the original Greek the word for "earth" is always preceded by the definite article.
[22] Bowman and Komoszewski, *Putting Jesus in His Place*, 2,368 of 4,522.
[23] Craig A. Evans, *Fabricating Jesus: How Modern Scholars Distort the Gospels* (Illinois: Inter Varsity Press, 2006), 149, Kindle edition; Craig A. Evans, *Matthew* (New York: Cambridge University Press, 2012), 200; Witherington, *The Christology of Jesus*, 246.
[24] Bowman and Komoszewski, *Putting Jesus in His Place*, 2,368 of 4,522; Evans, *Fabricating Jesus*, 149; Joseph S. Exell and Henry Donald Maurice Spence-Jones, *The Complete Pulpit Commentary. Volume 7. Matthew to John. A Exposition, Homiletics, and Homilies Commentary on the Bible* (Harrington, Delaware: Delmarva Publication, 2013), 19,360-19,372 of 161,039.

would have the same authority on earth that he received (or will receive) in heaven. Jesus thus essentially meant that his "authority includes forgiving sins, and that this may be exercised not only in the future and in 'the clouds of heaven,'" but it may be exercised even now "on earth." [25]

Mark 2:27-28: "The Sabbath was made for man, not man for the Sabbath. So the Son of Man is lord even of the Sabbath."

The very next pericope with a Son of Man saying represents one among the various Sabbath controversies that are included in the Gospels.[26] The religious leaders criticize Jesus for allowing his disciples to pick and eat heads of grain on the Sabbath, which they considered a violation of the Sabbath. Jesus answers in 2:25-26 that David had also broken the law in order to assuage his hunger and that of his companions, implying that Jesus could also do the same. In making an analogy with David, Jesus was using the Jewish interpretive principle that was called *gezera shawa* ("an equivalent regulation").[27]

The view that Sabbath was made as a gift for humankind "is common both in the OT and in early Jewish literature (Exod. 16:29; *Jub* 2:17; *Mekilta* 109B on Exod. 31:14)."[28] Jesus is evidently referring to himself in verse 28, but many scholars have interpreted the verse as a generic

---

[25] Exell and Spence-Jones, *The Complete Pulpit Commentary. Volume 7. Matthew to John. A Exposition, Homiletics, and Homilies Commentary on the Bible*, 19,372 of 161,039.
[26] Witherington, *The Gospel of Mark*, 1,926 of 7,980.
[27] Craig A. Evans, *Ancient Texts for New Testament Studies: A Guide to the Background Literature* (Minneapolis, Minnesota: Baker Academic, 2005), 219.
[28] Witherington, *The Gospel of Mark*, 1,967 of 7,980.

statement. One may interpret it as Jesus saying that because the Sabbath was put in place to benefit humankind, humankind is master of the Sabbath.[29] Although one may interpret the statement of verse 28 as generic, it more likely is a definite statement which exclusively refers to Jesus for several reasons. First, Jesus switches from the generic "man" in verse 27 to "the Son of Man" in the next verse. If he intended to make a generic statement in verse 28 as well, why did he not continue to say "man" as in the previous verse? Second, there is no instance in the *Tanakh* of "lord" being used generically for humankind as a whole or a group of people,[30] therefore the use of "lord" in Mark 2:28 should be taken as a reference to Jesus himself. Third, being given the gift of the Sabbath from God is not identical to "humans ruling the Sabbath or overruling some Sabbath regulations."[31] If the Sabbath was a gift to humankind, it is not necessarily follow that any man is lord of the Sabbath. For instance, God may have created the earth for human beings, but only God remains Lord of all creation (including the earth), whereas humans are only custodians. As in Mark 2:10, where Jesus claims the authority to forgive sins, here Jesus claims to have

---

[29] Vermes, *Jesus the Jew*, 180.

[30] Argument from Amaris Rivera (personal communication); Maurice Casey, *The Solution to the 'Son of Man' Problem* (New York: T & T Clark International, 2007), 4,416 of 6,420, Kindle edition; verified using *Accordance*. The ESV features 1,033 instances of "Lord" (with either a capital "L" or a lowercase "l") in the *Tanakh*. In each case the term is used in reference to either God or to a specific individual (usually a king, a prophet, or an angel) (*Accordance* and George V. Wigram, "Englishman's Concordance," *Bible Hub*, last accessed April 16, 2019, http://biblehub.com/hebrew/yahweh_3068.htm).

[31] Witherington, *The Gospel of Mark*, 1,982 of 7,980.

another authority, authority over the Sabbath.³² It is thus likely that both these accounts allude to Daniel 7:14 and the authority (or "dominion") given to the "son of man."³³

Mark 8:31: "And he began to teach them that the Son of Man must suffer many things and be rejected by the elders and the chief priests and the scribes and be killed, and after three days rise again."

In the Gospel of Mark, Jesus makes three main Passion predictions, the first appearing in Mark 8:31 (although in the form of indirect speech). The phrase "he began" "marks a turning point" in the Gospel and in Jesus' ministry.³⁴ In this chapter, Witherington states that "for the first time since 1:1, Jesus is designated the Christ" (translated from the Greek word which has the equivalent Hebrew word translated as "Messiah").³⁵ "After that recognition comes, a dramatic change in tone happens in the story. From then on the focus is on Jesus as the suffering Son of Man."³⁶

It is undeniable that in their current context Jesus' prophecies about the looming suffering, death, and resurrection of the Son of Man, refer to him and him alone. But prophecies are problematic, for it would require one to presuppose that predictive prophecy is possible and that the dead can be brought back to life. As a result, scholars often dismiss them as *vaticinia ex eventu*, prophecies that were put on Jesus' lips after the events transpired. The belief, however, is

---

[32] Witherington, *The Gospel of Mark*, 1,992 of 7,980.
[33] Ibid.
[34] *NLT Parallel Study Bible*, 1,782.
[35] Witherington, *The Gospel of Mark*, 3,572 of 7,980; Daniel Boyarin, *The Jewish Gospels: The Story of the Jewish Christ* (New York: The New Press, 2012 (the paperback edition I used was published in 2013)), 26.
[36] Witherington, *The Gospel of Mark*, 3,572 of 7,980.

grounded in Scripture, for the Bible has numerous examples of prophets who throughout Israel's history made statements about future events, including predicting someone's death. Of course, they are often considered *vaticinia ex eventu* as well. The belief in the resurrection of the dead, also rooted in Scripture, was a widely held Jewish belief at the time of Jesus (though to what extent is uncertain). The Pharisees, who are often mentioned in the Gospels, were known for their belief in the resurrection of the dead.[37] At least with regards to Jesus' death, Craig Blomberg affirms that "given the volatile days in which Jesus lived, even an uninspired person might have successfully predicted" it.[38]

The theme of suffering followed by exaltation or vindication is central to Daniel.[39] Actually, one may argue that virtually all of the books of the Bible follow a "U-shaped" pattern of tribulation followed by exaltation.[40] Jesus, whose Passion predictions also correspond to the "U-shaped structure of descent and ascent,"[41] sums up the theme himself

---

[37] Acts 23:8.
[38] Craig L. Blomberg, *Jesus and the Gospels: An Introduction and Survey* (Nashville, Tennessee: B&H Publishing Group, 2009), 4,003 of 14,489, Kindle edition.
[39] C. K. Barrett, "The Background of Mark 10:45," in *New Testament Essays: Studies in Memory of T. W. Manson 1893-1958*, ed. A. J. B. Higgins (Manchester, UK: The University Press, 1959), 13-14; John J. Collins, *The Scepter and the Star: Messianism in the Light of the Dead Sea Scrolls* (Michigan and Cambridge, UK: Wm. B. Eerdmans Publishing Co., 2010), 177.
[40] Northrop Frye, *The Great Code: The Bible and Literature* (New York/San Diego, California: A Harvest/ HBJ Book, 1983 ed.), 169.
[41] Regina M. Schwartz, *The Curse of Cain: The Violent Legacy of Monotheism* (Chicago: The University of Chicago Press, 1997), 167-168; quotation (in slightly different form) originally from Regina M. Schwartz, "Joseph's Bones and the Resurrection of the Text: Remembering in the Bible," *PMLA* 103, no. 2 (March, 1988): 115, published by Modern Language

succinctly: "whoever humbles himself will be exalted."[42] Although it is a constant theme throughout the Bible, the book of Daniel also has distinctive features that make it more likely that the underlying theme of the Passion predictions and the prophecies themselves were rooted particularly in Daniel. For one, Daniel in particular presents faithful Israelites who are sentenced to death, but who are miraculously rescued by God.[43] First the prophet Daniel's friends, refusing to worship Nebuchadnezzar's statue as ordered by the king, are thrown into a blazing furnace, but are then miraculously rescued. Afterwards, Daniel refuses to stop praying to God as was prohibited by the Persians, and is thrown into a den of lions before being miraculously rescued himself, without even a scratch on him. "All previous 'rescues' of God's people in Daniel (e.g., 3:28; 6:27) had foreshadowed, and now culminated in, the resurrection from the dead (12:2-3)."[44]

      The books of Daniel—and Isaiah—are two of the few books of the *Tanakh* that explicitly refer to the general resurrection of the dead.[45] Concerning the resurrection, Daniel 12:2 states: "And many of those who sleep in the dust of the earth shall awake, some to everlasting life, and some to shame and everlasting contempt." Daniel is himself reassured of a future resurrection in the book's final verse: "But go your

---

Association, last accessed April 7, 2019, JSTOR, https://www.jstor.org/stable/462428.

[42] Matthew 23:12.

[43] See *NLT Parallel Study Bible*, 1,531-1,532; 1,562.

[44] *NLT Parallel Study Bible*, 1,562.

[45] Ibid.: concerning the resurrection "see also Job 19:25-26; Ps 16:10; and Isa 26:19."

way till the end. And you shall rest and shall stand in your allotted place at the end of the days."[46]

One can thus understand that the underlying theme of Jesus' predictions may have been primarily made on the basis of Daniel because of the specific reference to the resurrection.[47] The book guarantees that the saints of God would one day come back to life, a prediction which would have included Jesus. Although people did not expect someone to be resurrected on the third day or before everyone else, Christians consider Jesus to have been the "founder" and the "firstborn from the dead,"[48] meaning Jesus' resurrection would be counted as the first of the general resurrection of the end times, not one apart from it.[49] Jesus would have thus been demonstrating the reality of the resurrection prophesized in Daniel 12:2-3. And just "as Jesus was raised from the dead and made immortal, so also will his followers."[50]

It must be noted that although his followers would suffer in a *similar* manner, the Passion predictions in Mark cannot be including his disciples, for not all of them were killed (e.g., the Apostle John), and evidently none of them were resurrected on the third day. The Son of Man saying itself is not generic, but by pronouncing the saying Jesus was

---

[46] 12:13.
[47] Jane Schaberg, "Daniel 7, 12 and the New Testament Passion-Resurrection Predictions," *New Testament Studies* 31, no.2 (1985): 213.
[48] Respectively, Hebrews 12:2 and Colossians 1:18 (see also Acts 26:23 and Revelation 1:5).
[49] Bowman and Komoszewski, *Putting Jesus in His Place*, 2,562 of 4,522.
[50] Adela Yarboro Collins and John J. Collins, *King and Messiah as Son of God: Divine, Human, and Angelic Messianic Figures in Biblical and Related Literature* (Michigan: Wm. B. Eerdmans Publishing Co., 2008), 108. See 1 Corinthians 15:23.

making an implication that his disciples would suffer as well by following him.[51]

    Mark 8:38: "For whoever is ashamed of me and of my words in this adulterous and sinful generation, of him will the Son of Man also be ashamed when he comes in the glory of his Father with the holy angels."

Whereas the Son of Man previously had to undergo great suffering, he will be exalted in the future, coming on this occasion in "glory." Once more, Daniel 7:13-14 is indirectly alluded to: "with the clouds of heaven there came one like a son of man, and he came to the Ancient of Days and was presented before him. And to him was given dominion and glory and a kingdom …"[52] The Markan verse alludes to the Danielic "son of man," and "in the glory of his Father" may be alluding to 7:14, for the Danielic "son of man" receives "glory" from the Ancient of Days.

By using the word "ashamed," Jesus may have implied that the Son of Man would come in judgment,[53] and thus that the Danielic figure was also given the authority to judge by the Ancient of Days.[54] The 1st century CE texts of *Similitudes* and *4 Ezra* take for granted that the Messiah is

---

[51] Morna Dorothy Hooker, "Is the Son of Man Problem Really Insoluble?" In *Text and Interpretation: Studies in the New Testament Presented to Matthew Black*, ed. Ernest Best and R.McL. Wilson (Cambridge, UK: Cambridge University Press, 1979), 165; Witherington, *The Christology of Jesus*, 249.
[52] Daniel 7:13-14.
[53] Edward A. McDowell, *Son of Man and Suffering Servant: A Historical and Exegetical Study of Synoptic Narratives Revealing the Consciousness of Jesus Concerning His Person and Mission* (Tennessee: Broadman Press, 1946 3rd printing), 115.
[54] Bowman and Komoszewski, *Putting Jesus in His Place*, 2,362 of 4,522.

given authority to judge.[55] The pre-Christian Qumranic texts of *11QMelchizedek* and the *Aramaic Apocalypse* also give their Messianic figures the role of judgment.[56] In Daniel, this may be suggested by 7:10 (which states that "the court sat in judgment"), as well as by the overall context of the seventh chapter, in which judgment of the beasts and vindication of the saints both take place.[57] Also, if the Danielic "son of man" had the authority to forgive sins, it would not be implausible if he also had the authority to judge, for the one "who judges also absolves."[58] Thus it is more likely that Jesus meant that the Son of Man would be assuming the role of a judge, rather than that of a mere witness,[59] if the Son of Man already had the authority to forgive sins. The Son of Man's role in judgment is made more explicit for instance in Matthew 16:27: "For the Son of Man is going to come with his angels in the glory of his Father, and then he will repay each person according to what he has done."

It is rather clear that Jesus was talking about a specific Son of Man, but some scholars have postulated that Jesus was referring to another individual who would come in the future. It is unlikely, however, that Jesus would be predicting

---

[55] Collins, *The Scepter and the Star*, 213; Michael E. Stone, "The Messiah in 4 Ezra," *Judaisms and Their Messiahs at the Turn of the Christian Era*, ed. Jacob Neusner et al. (New York: Cambridge University Press, 1987), 212.
[56] Collins, *The Scepter and the Star*, 178 and 195.
[57] Bowman and Komoszewski, *Putting Jesus in His Place*, 2,362 of 4,522.
[58] Tertullian, in "The Five Books Against Marcion," Book IV, Chapter X, Dr. Holmes, trans., in *Ante-Nicene Fathers Volume 3*, by Philip Schaff, ed. Allan Menzies (Michigan: Wm. B. Eerdmans Publishing Co., originally published in 1885), 20,410 of 45,166, Kindle edition.
[59] For instance, Casey argues that Jesus was implying that he would have the role of a "crucial witness," not that of a judge (Casey, *The Solution to the 'Son of Man' Problem*, 3,159 of 6,420).

the coming of another Son of Man figure, for that was precisely John the Baptist's role: he was preparing for the arrival of the Lord,[60] not for another John the Baptist! Bultmann, in particular, stated that in the Son of Man sayings Jesus originally meant someone else, but that they were later added in contexts in which it would be evident that he was referring to himself.[61] However, the New Testament provides no evidence elsewhere that Jesus was expecting any other Son of Man other than himself to come sometime in the future.[62] Moreover, around Jesus' time, it would probably not have been surprising for Galileans to refer to themselves in the third person in Aramaic, or to switch from first person to third even in mid-sentence.[63] This may well be indicated by the Targums, in which there are over 100 instances of self-reference in the third person in Aramaic (although not with the expression "son of man").[64] One may thus assume that Mark 8:38 is referring solely to Jesus, as are all the other Son of Man sayings up to this point in the Gospel.

---

[60] Mark 1:3.

[61] Rudolf Bultmann, *The History of the Synoptic Tradition*, John Marsh, trans. (New York and Evanston: Harper & Row, 1968, 2nd ed), 122.

[62] Witherington, *The Christology of Jesus*, 257.

[63] Alejandro Díez Macho, "La Cristología del Hijo del Hombre y el Uso de la Tercera Persona en Vez de la Primera," *Scripta Theologica* 14, no. 1 (January 1, 1982): 195 and 200, last accessed January 22, 2014, ATLA Religion Database with ATLASerials, EBSCOhost.

[64] Ibid. Regarding the Targums, " the extant manuscripts and the traditions underlying them range in date from NT times to well into the Middle Ages" (Evans, *Ancient Texts for New Testament Studies*, 187).

Mark 9:9: "And as they were coming down the mountain, he charged them to tell no one what they had seen, until the Son of Man had risen from the dead."

This verse and Mark 8:31 are the only two verses in indirect speech in the Gospel. It is clear from context that the verse refers to Jesus alone, and it can also be said that the prediction was rooted in Daniel (but not Daniel alone) because of "Son of Man" and Jesus' reference to his resurrection.

Mark 9:12: "Elijah does come first to restore all things. And how is it written of the Son of Man that he should suffer many things and be treated with contempt?"

This saying was part of an answer to the disciples' question of whether Elijah had to appear first, in the pericope of Jesus' Transfiguration. Again the verse is referring only to Jesus, indicated by context, for the saying is part of a response in which Jesus is referring to his forerunner John the Baptist, who came "in the spirit and power of Elijah."[65] Bultmann considered this verse as an interpolation, and that Jesus was referring to someone else.[66] Again, however, there is no evidence in the New Testament to even suggest that Jesus meant another person other than himself.[67]

On this occasion, more than the book of Daniel (or other books of the *Tanakh*), Jesus may have had the book of Isaiah in mind.[68] Several scholars have posited that in Mark, Jesus was combining the "son of man" from Daniel with

---

[65] Luke 1:17.
[66] Rudolf Bultmann, *The History of the Synoptic Tradition*, 125.
[67] Witherington, *The Christology of Jesus*, 257.
[68] Joachim Jeremias, *New Testament Theology* (New York: Charles Scribner's Sons, 1971), 286.

Isaiah's account of the "Suffering Servant" in Isaiah 52:13-53:12.[69] In Second Temple Judaism, the "Suffering Servant" may have had a Messianic interpretation,[70] but the interpretation was not universal, for even in Acts 8:30-35, Philip is asked whether Isaiah the prophet was referring to himself or some other person.[71] Jesus quotes from or alludes to Isaiah around forty times in the Synoptic Gospels,[72] therefore it would not have been out of character for him to have alluded to Isaiah here as well.[73] In this verse, Jesus may be specifically alluding to Isaiah 53:3: "He was despised and rejected by men, a man of sorrows and acquainted with grief."

Mark 9:31: "The Son of Man is going to be delivered into the hands of men, and they will kill him. And when he is killed, after three days he will rise"

This verse constitutes Jesus' second prediction concerning his Passion. Though instead of saying that "the Son of Man" would suffer, Jesus said that "the Son of Man is going to be delivered into the hands of men," a phrase which

---

[69] See Boyarin, *The Jewish Gospels*, 141; Burkett, *The Son of Man Debate*, 47; Rudolf Bultmann, *Theology of the New Testament* (New York: Charles Scribner's Sons, 1951), 31; S.E. Johnson, "Son of Man," in *Interpreter's Dictionary of the Bible*, Volume 4 (New York/ Tennessee: Abingdon Press, 1962), 415.
[70] William Horbury, *Jewish Messianism and the Cult of Christ* (London, UK: SCM Press Ltd, 1998), 33.
[71] Horbury, *Jewish Messianism and the Cult of Christ*, 33.
[72] Evans, *Fabricating Jesus*, 39.
[73] Ibid.

is included in all the Synoptic Gospels (though with minor variations).[74]

One may argue that this Markan verse echoes Daniel 7:25: "the saints of the Most High … they shall be given into his hand for a time, times, and half a time."[75] Jane Schaberg identified three similarities between this Danielic verse and the Markan verse: (1) the use of the future passive; (2) the occurrence of "into…hand(s)"; (3) a time indication: "a time, times, and half a time" would correspond to the "after three days" of the Markan verse.[76] In the *Tanakh*, there are 70 verses that simultaneously contain "delivered" (or "given") and "into … hand(s)."[77] The only verse that has the future passive, and that also after (1) and (2) is followed by some form of time indication, is precisely Daniel 7:25. The only other verse that approximates the three similarities outlined by Schaberg is Jeremiah 32:24, but it does not feature the future passive (it states "is given"), for the verse is describing an event that is already taking place (not one which *will* occur), as indicated by the end of the verse: "What you spoke has come to pass, and behold, you see it." Yet it is the mysterious time reference that is key in distinguishing Daniel 7:25 from the other verses of the *Tanakh*. Thus, the similarities—taken together—may indicate that Jesus was

---

[74] Jamieson et al., "Commentary Critical and Explanatory on the Whole Bible," *Christian Classics Ethereal Library*, last accessed April 26, 2019, http://www.ccel.org/ccel/jamieson/jfb.txt, 1871. See Matthew 17:22, Luke 9:44, and Luke 24:7.
[75] Schaberg, "Daniel 7, 12 and the New Testament Passion-Resurrection Predictions," 213.
[76] Ibid.
[77] *Accordance*. In the 70 verses, "delivered" and "given" are idiomatically equivalent.

deliberately evoking Daniel 7:25,[78] although in the most subtle way. Jesus may have been evoking that verse in order to pronounce a prediction regarding himself that paralleled that of the saints in 7:25, but Jesus may have also identified himself in the prophecy in Daniel 7:25.

The prophecy in Daniel 7:25 is sufficiently vague that it could have corresponded to more than one historical event or time period. Daniel 7:25 indicates that God's saints would undergo a period of tribulation before inheriting the kingdom, thus the verse could also imply that the "son of man," the Saint of saints, would not be exempt from suffering before inheriting his crown.[79] Jesus may have thus seen himself as one of "the saints of the Most High,"[80] though the chief one among them, as *the* "Holy One of God."[81] Just as Jesus would have been the first to be raised from the dead, he also would have been the first to suffer and die under the new covenant.[82]

Also, עדן (*iddan*), the Aramaic word for "time" in "time, times, and half a time," could correspond to any length of time (whether a day, a week, or a year).[83] Even within Daniel, the time reference is variously interpreted: in 8:14, it is

---

[78] Schaberg, "Daniel 7, 12 and the New Testament Passion-Resurrection Predictions," 213.
[79] Hooker, "Is the Son of Man Problem Really Insoluble?", 160-161, 166. *NLT Parallel Study Bible*, 1,782; Schaberg, "Daniel 7, 12 and the New Testament Passion-Resurrection Predictions," 208.
[80] Daniel 7:25.
[81] John 6:69 (see also Mark 1:24 and Luke 4:34).
[82] *NLT Parallel Study Bible*, 1,782.
[83] See Joseph S. Exell and Henry Donald Maurice Spence-Jones, *The Complete Pulpit Commentary. Volume 5. Isaiah to Daniel. A Exposition, Homiletics, and Homilies Commentary on the Bible* (Harrington, Delaware: Delmarva Publication, 2013), 141,004 of 149,269.

interpreted as "2,300 evenings and mornings"; but in 12:11, it is interpreted as "1,290 days".[84] Moreover, in the book of Revelation, the time indication is interpreted as "1,260 days,"[85] meaning that the interpretations were not limited only to the ones stated in Daniel. The mysterious phrase "time, times, and half a time" could thus correspond to any length of time between the affliction and suffering of the saints and their exaltation.

The account of Revelation 11:1-14, predicts that two eschatological prophets will be killed and resurrected after "three and a half days."[86] The account states that once the prophets have died, "after the three and a half days a breath of life from God entered them, and they stood up on their feet, and great fear fell on those who saw them."[87] The account evidently brings to mind Jesus' own death and resurrection, but the "half" in the time lapse between the two prophets' death and resurrection-ascension provides a hint that the 3.5 days represent an interpretation of the Danielic time reference.[88] Also, the 3.5 days parallel the 3.5 years ("1,260 days"[89]) stated in the same account. The "time, and times, and half a time" in 12:14 is precisely interpreted as 3.5 years ("1,260 days") in 12:6 of the book of Revelation.[90] In a similar manner, one may argue that earlier Jesus had

---

[84] Schaberg, "Daniel 7, 12 and the New Testament Passion-Resurrection Predictions," 209.
[85] Revelation 12:6.
[86] Revelation 11:9, 11.
[87] Revelation 11:11.
[88] Schaberg, "Daniel 7, 12 and the New Testament Passion-Resurrection Predictions," 210.
[89] Revelation 11:3.
[90] "Time, times and half a time" occurs in 12:14 in Revelation. It occurs in 7:25 and 12:7 in Daniel.

interpreted the Danielic time reference himself, and had applied it to the period of his Passion.[91]

Jesus perhaps had earlier himself interpreted the days between his crucifixion and his resurrection in a similar manner, but instead of interpreting the "times" as days, Jesus perhaps had interpreted the "times" in terms of number nighttime and daytime periods (each representing 12 hours). For instance, Daniel 8:14 interprets the time reference in 7:25 as "2,300 evenings and mornings," which "could refer to a period of 1,150 days (1,150 evenings + 1,150 mornings, about 3½ years) or 2,300 days."[92] At the time, it was the Jewish custom to always divide "the day, from sun-rising to sun-setting, into twelve equal parts; but these parts, or hours, were longer or shorter, according to the different seasons of the year."[93] Thus a daytime or nighttime period was always 12 "hours," regardless of the time of the season. In that case, Jesus perhaps interpreted the Danielic time reference—that would have been applied to the time between his crucifixion and his resurrection—as 3.5 "evenings and mornings" (or 3.5 12-hour cycles): 1 daytime period, 2 nighttime periods, and half a daytime period (on the day of his crucifixion). The general consensus among scholars is that "after three days" and "on the third day"[94] were idiomatically equivalent in

---

[91] See Boyarin, *The Jewish Gospels*, 44, 144-145; Schaberg, "Daniel 7, 12 and the New Testament Passion-Resurrection Predictions," 215.
[92] *NLT Parallel Study Bible*, 1,554.
[93] Adam Clarke, "Commentary on John 11:9," "The Adam Clarke Commentary," *SudyLight.org*, last accessed April 22, 2019, https://www.studylight.org/commentaries/acc/john-11.html, 1832.
[94] E.g., Luke 9:22.

antiquity,[95] and one would start counting the day of his crucifixion as the first day. The 3.5 "evenings and mornings" would then have been equivalent to "three days" in idiomatic Aramaic.

Jesus refers to his resurrection in this Markan verse, which again may be alluding to—though not exclusively—Daniel 12:1-2.[96] Following his sufferings, Jesus predicts his vindication and exaltation through his resurrection in this Markan verse. In the same way, in Daniel the affliction predicted for the saints of God in 7:25 is followed by their vindication in the following two verses, with their ultimate exaltation being their future resurrection on Judgment Day (stated in Daniel 12:1-3),[97] a resurrection "to everlasting life."[98] Yet while the resurrection of the saints has yet to take place, the resurrection of Jesus occurred "after three days."[99]

As a result, not only are the themes in the Son of Man sayings linked with those of Daniel, but the prophecies themselves arguably "correspond to Daniel's prophecies."[100] Jesus' reference to the resurrection, combined with the threefold similarity to Daniel 7:25 and the expression "Son of Man" being derived from Daniel 7:13, indicate that Jesus was deliberately—though subtly—establishing a connection with

---

[95] Norman Walker, "After Three Days," *Novum Testamentum* 4, no. 4 (December 1, 1960): 261, last accessed February 27, 2014, ATLA Religion Database with ATLASerials, EBSCOhost.
[96] Schaberg, "Daniel 7, 12 and the New Testament Passion-Resurrection Predictions," 211, 213.
[97] Ibid., 219.
[98] Daniel 12:2.
[99] Hooker, "Is the Son of Man Problem Really Insoluble?", 165.
[100] *NLT Parallel Study Bible*, 1,782.

Daniel.[101] However, whereas the prediction in Daniel 7:25 refers to all of God's saints, Jesus made a prediction in Mark 9:31 that could be applied only to himself. Also, whereas Daniel 12 refers to the general resurrection (which would include Jesus as the "the first to rise from the dead"[102]), Jesus in this Markan verse refers only to his own.

Mark 10:33-34: "See, we are going up to Jerusalem, and the Son of Man will be delivered over to the chief priests and the scribes, and they will condemn him to death and deliver him over to the Gentiles. And they will mock him and spit on him, and flog him and kill him. And after three days he will rise."

Jesus' third prediction, which he stated when nearing Jerusalem, was the most detailed of all. As with the previous prediction, Jesus may have been alluding to Daniel 7:25 and 12:1-2. The fact that Jesus' predictions are not expressed in more precise terms makes it more likely the prophecies were genuinely pronounced by Jesus.[103] Although this prediction is Jesus' most precise one, Jesus says that he would be handed over to "the Gentiles," not to Pontius Pilate.[104] In Mark, he also says that he would be killed, not that he would be crucified.[105] Neither does he say that he would rise specifically the day after the Sabbath of Passover. The indefiniteness in his prediction is characteristic of Jesus, who avoids making overly explicit pronouncements in the Gospel. For instance, during the last Passover dinner with the Twelve, after

---

[101] Schaberg, "Daniel 7, 12 and the New Testament Passion-Resurrection Predictions," 213.
[102] Acts 26:23.
[103] Witherington, *The Gospel of Mark*, 4,049 of 7,980.
[104] Ibid.
[105] Ibid.

predicting that one of them would betray him, Jesus avoids referring to Judas explicitly by name.[106]

Mark 10:45: "For even the Son of Man came not to be served but to serve, and to give his life as a ransom for many."

Mark 10:33-34 mentions the forthcoming death of the Son of Man, but in this verse Jesus explained the purpose of his death.[107] The verb is in the past tense, indicating that the Son of Man already came, and it would be difficult to interpret this saying as corresponding to anyone except Jesus. There may be an implicit allusion to Daniel 7:13-14 due to the adverb "even" and Jesus' use of the word "served." "Even" implies that it was contrary to expectation, meaning that contrary to what one might expect, the Danielic "son of man" came not to be "served," but to be at the service of others.[108] What Jesus probably meant was that the Son of Man would not be served in the way Gentile rulers demanded to be served (Mark 10:42), but in a way that was diametrically opposed: "Jesus contrasted the world's leadership style—military power, coercion, and bribery—with his own servant leadership in sacrificing himself for others."[109] In Jesus' emblematic paradoxical style, it seems that he essentially meant that one of the best ways to serve the Son of Man was to serve others.

The Greek word translated as "ransom" in the 10:45 is "a mercantile term" and "refers to the deliverance by purchase of a slave or prisoner of war or of some object one

---

[106] Mark 14:18-20.
[107] Witherington, *The Gospel of Mark*, 4,377 of 7,980.
[108] Witherington, *The Christology of Jesus*, 262.
[109] *NLT Parallel Study Bible*, 1,960.

wants back (see Lev. 25:47-55)."[110] Therefore when Jesus said that the Son of Man would "give his life as a ransom for many," he probably meant he was offering it as a substitutionary sacrifice to atone the sins "of many."[111] Jesus seems to have made an allusion to Isaiah 53:11-12, but because of the Markan verse's "servant language,"[112] the account of the "Suffering Servant" as a whole also forms a basis for Jesus' saying, an account which—with Daniel—serves as a basis for the Son of Man sayings.[113] Although the idea of the Son of Man suffering and being killed could have been derived from Daniel alone, the combination with Isaiah may have been necessary to explain the *reason* for the Son of Man's affliction and death.[114] Isaiah mentions a sin offering in 53:10 instead of a ransom, but Mark 10:45 and Isaiah 53:10 both suggest a substitutionary sacrifice.[115] By indicating that the Son of Man's death would be salvific for others, the verse cannot be interpreted as generic, for not anyone can atone for people's sins.

Mark 13:26-27: "And then they will see the Son of Man coming in clouds with great power and glory. And then he will send out the angels and gather his elect from the four winds, from the ends of the earth to the ends of heaven."

Jesus utters this saying during in the Olivet Discourse, a saying in which Jesus again mentions a future Son of Man, who will return with "great power and glory." The "elect"

---

[110] Witherington, *The Gospel of Mark*, 4,379 of 7,980.
[111] Isaiah 53:12.
[112] Witherington, *The Gospel of Mark*, 4,339-4,374 of 7,980
[113] Ibid.; *NLT Parallel Study Bible*, 1,856.
[114] Jeremias, *New Testament Theology*, 286-288.
[115] Witherington, *The Gospel of Mark*, 4,342 of 7,980.

belong to the Son of Man (they are "his,"[116]), therefore from the verse one can infer that the saying was referring only to Jesus, given that it cannot be said that God's "elect" can belong to human beings in general (or to any human being). As with Mark 8:38, Jesus may be implying that the Son of Man would be coming with the authority to judge.[117]

Mark 14:21: "For the Son of Man goes as it is written of him, but woe to that man by whom the Son of Man is betrayed! It would have been better for that man if he had not been born."

Jesus could have been referring to all the passages of Scripture that predicted the Son of Man's death when he said, "as it is written of him." From context, Jesus is evidently speaking about himself, for he is referring to his betrayal by Judas. If taken completely out of context, perhaps the saying *could* be interpreted as generic, but it is highly unlikely that Jesus meant to merely make a general statement about man dying and being betrayed.[118] This is the case with many Son of Man sayings in the Gospels, which when completely removed from their narrative or historical contexts *could* perhaps be interpreted as generic, but even when taken out of

---

[116] John Parsons, "Yeshua is LORD," *Hebrew for Christians*, last accessed April 23, 2019, www.hebrew4christians.com/Names_of_G-d/Yeshua_is_Adonai/yeshua_is_adonai.htm.

[117] Benjamin E. Reynolds, "The Use of the Son of Man Idiom in the Gospel of John," in *'Who is This Son of Man?': The Latest Scholarship on a Puzzling Expression of the Historical Jesus*, ed. Larry W. Hurtado and Paul L. Owen et al. (New York: Bloomsbury T & T Clark, 2011), 125.

[118] Paul L. Owen, "Problems with Casey's 'Solution'," in *'Who is This Son of Man?': The Latest Scholarship on a Puzzling Expression of the Historical Jesus*, ed. Larry W. Hurtado and Paul L. Owen et al. (New York: Bloomsbury T & T Clark, 2011), 45; analogous argument in Hooker, "Is the Son of Man Problem Really Insoluble?", 158.

context, the interpretation of the Son of Man as a title of a specific person would nevertheless not be excluded.[119]

Mark 14:41: "Are you still sleeping and taking your rest? It is enough; the hour has come. The Son of Man is betrayed into the hands of sinners."

Mark 14:41 was Jesus' last prediction (though not a full Passion prediction), a saying which was spoken in Gethsemane, right when he was about to get arrested (hence the present tense of "is betrayed"). Again, the verse can only be pointing to Jesus.

Mark 14:62: "And Jesus said, 'I am, and you will see the Son of Man seated at the right hand of Power, and coming with the clouds of heaven.'"

Shortly after his arrest, Jesus pronounces his final Son of Man saying in Mark before the Jewish priests and teachers. In Mark 14:62, Jesus makes his most explicit reference to Daniel 7:13 after having stated that his "hour" had "come" in the previous Son of Man saying. Whereas before Jesus sometimes combined the Danielic "son of man" with the "Suffering Servant" of Isaiah, Jesus' answer combines it with Psalm 110, specifically verses 1 and 5:[120]

---

[119] Burkett, *The Son of Man Debate*, 96.
[120] Darrell L. Bock, "The Use of Daniel 7 in Jesus' Trial, with Implications for his Self-Understanding," in *'Who is This Son of Man?': The Latest Scholarship on a Puzzling Expression of the Historical Jesus*, ed. Larry W. Hurtado and Paul L. Owen et al. (New York: Bloomsbury T & T Clark, 2011), 82; Robert D. Rowe, "Is Daniel's 'Son of Man' Messianic?" In *Christ the Lord: Studies in Christology presented to Donald Guthrie*, ed. Harold H. Rowdon (Leicester, UK: Inter-Varsity Press, 1982), 71. Rowe states that "the only place in the Old Testament where any individual is represented as being enthroned by the side of God is Psalm 110:1."

> The LORD says to my Lord: "Sit at my right hand, until I make your enemies your footstool."[121]
>
> The Lord is at your right hand.[122]

Jesus had already introduced Psalm 110 when teaching at the Temple, but before the Sanhedrin he explicitly applies it to himself.[123] Jesus interprets the "Lord" at God's right hand as the Messiah, as is implied in the pericope of Mark 12:35-37.[124] Jesus tells the Pharisees that "David himself calls him Lord,"[125] with the implication that "him" is the Messiah. Given that the "Lord" in Psalm 110 is implicitly interpreted as the Messiah by Jesus, one may infer that for Jesus, the Son of Man who sits at God's right hand is the Messiah.[126]

The statement in Mark 14:62 thus cannot be a generic one, for there can be only one Messiah (or at least there is no evidence in the New Testament to suggest that there was another one).[127] Jesus is also referring to himself—not another future Son of Man—for he responds affirmatively with "I am." That this verse with the exalted Son of Man refers to Jesus also confirms that the other verses regarding the exalted Son of Man—Mark 8:38 and 13:26—also refer to him.

---

[121] Psalm 110:1.
[122] Psalm 110:5.
[123] Bock, "The Use of Daniel 7 in Jesus' Trial," 82-83; Cf. Bowman and Komoszewski, *Putting Jesus in His Place*, 2,724 of 4,522.
[124] Bowman and Komoszewski, *Putting Jesus in His Place*, 2,727 of 4,522.
[125] Mark 12:37
[126] Cf. Boyarin, *The Jewish Gospels*, 137; Collins and Collins, *King and Messiah as Son of God*, 133.
[127] Collins and Collins, *King and Messiah as Son of God*, 133.

However, whereas the other parallel Son of Man sayings are nearly identical, Jesus is asked two separate questions in Luke's parallel account instead of the one in Mark, although Jesus responds essentially in the same way. It seems necessary then to take into account the other parallel sayings in this particular case. Sometimes a Gospel might have Jesus' *ipsissima verba* (his exact words), while another might have Jesus' *vox* ("voice," the gist of what he said) in a parallel saying.[128] Here it may be that Jesus' exact words are a form of combination of the parallel sayings, with each account preserving his actual words, but no one account preserving *all* of the words Jesus actually said.[129] Jesus' actual exchange with the Sanhedrin may have been slightly more extended than the one in Mark.[130] The following exchange represents an attempt at harmonizing the parallel accounts of Mark 14:61-64, Matthew 26:63-65, and Luke 22:67-71:

> The high priest said to him, "I adjure you by the living God, tell us if you are the Christ."
> Jesus said to them, "If I tell you, you will not believe, and if I ask you, you will not answer. But I tell you, from now on you will see the Son of Man seated at the right hand of Power, and coming with the clouds of heaven."
> So they all said, "Are you the Son of the Blessed, then?"
> Jesus replied, "You say that I am."

---

[128] Bock, *Studying the Historical Jesus*, 3,900 of 4,412.
[129] See Bock, *Studying the Historical Jesus*, 3,881 of 4,412.
[130] See Bock, *Studying the Historical Jesus*, 3,881 of 4,412.

Jesus responds affirmatively, but in a roundabout manner.[131] The Sanhedrin may have actually asked first if he was the Messiah, and then if he was God's Son, as in the Gospel of Luke. Jesus calling himself "the Son of Man" was probably not considered to be blasphemy at the time he said it, for the religious leaders had never accused Jesus of blasphemy despite having heard him use the term multiple times beforehand in their presence.[132] They probably understood "seated at the right hand of Power" as a Messianic claim, but probably still wanted a more explicit affirmation, which Jesus gave them after they asked if he was the Son of God ("You say that I am.").[133]

As a result, throughout the Gospel of Mark, in every single Son of Man saying, Jesus refers exclusively to himself, with Jesus also undoubtedly referring each time to the "son of man" from Daniel 7:13. In addition to directly alluding to Daniel 7:13, various details of each Son of Man saying imply that Jesus may have had the Danielic figure in mind when uttering the sayings.[134] One could also argue that major themes and ideas from the book of Daniel form a basis for the Markan Son of Man sayings, and that the sayings form a coherent whole on the basis of the thematic content of Daniel.[135] At the same time, Isaiah seems to have also been a

---

[131] Witherington, *The Christology of Jesus*, 260.
[132] *NLT Parallel Study Bible*, 1,875.
[133] Cf. Joel Marcus, "Mark 14:61: 'Are you the Messiah-Son-of-God?'" *Novum Testamentum* 31, no. 2 (April 1, 1989): 138-141, last accessed September 28, 2013, ATLA Religion Database with ATLASerials, EBSCOhost.
[134] Bock, *Studying the Historical Jesus*, 4,130 of 4,412.
[135] Ben Witherington, III, *The Christology of Jesus* (Minneapolis, Minnesota: Fortress Press, 1990), 245.

basis for Jesus' Son of Man sayings.[136] Jesus' Son of Man sayings, which have an underlying theme of initial suffering and loss followed by restoration and exaltation, are grounded especially in Daniel and Isaiah as a whole, which feature that theme constantly and refer specifically to the resurrection of the dead. There is thus no contradiction in affirming that the suffering Son of Man and the exalted Son of Man are one and the same person. As Witherington affirms, Jesus "saw himself taking on the role of Israel's representative, both at the last judgment before God and presently as the representative of suffering Israel on earth."[137]

Given that he was speaking only about himself when identifying with the "son of man" from Daniel 7:13, it follows that Jesus interpreted the Danielic "son of man" as an individual, not as a symbol for the people of Israel. The Danielic "son of man" is described in 7:14 as being the ruler of an eternal kingdom given to him by God. Yet by definition a title is "a name that describes someone's position or job."[138] Jesus identified with the Danielic "son of man," and thereby with his "job": by referring to the figure, Jesus was indirectly signaling his own office. In addition, as Timothée Colani stated, Jesus was continually saying things to the effect that "the Son of Man *came* to serve, … that he has the *authority* to forgive, or that he *must* be delivered to his enemies and be put to death. This expression designates therefore the office of which his Father found him worthy."[139] "The Son of Man"

---

[136] Jeremias, *New Testament Theology*, 286.
[137] Witherington, *The Christology of Jesus*, 269.
[138] *The New Oxford American Dictionary* (New York: Oxford University Press, Inc. e-book, 2010), 975,126 of 1,082,596, Kindle edition.
[139] Timothée Colani, *Jésus-Christ et les Croyances Messianiques de Son Temps* (Strasbourg, France: Treuttel Et Wurtz, Librairies- Editeurs, 1864), 117.

on Jesus' lips was thus "both titular and circumlocutionary."[140] The use of the title in the third person was not inconsistent with Jesus' mode of self-reference because in the Gospels, Jesus does not only refer to himself in the third person with the title of Son of Man.[141] Specifically in Mark, Jesus refers to himself in the third person as "Christ" in 9:41and as "the Son" in Mark 13:32.[142] Yet when Jesus was referring to himself as "the Son of Man," he was not only using it as a title, but, as most clearly indicated in Mark 14:62, he was also using it as a Messianic title.

B. The Son of Man as a Messianic Title
1. Jesus Used the Son of Man as a Messianic Title

Once the "son of man" is interpreted to be an individual, it seems inevitable to interpret the figure as the Messiah as well, even though this is not explicitly stated in Daniel.[143] The kingdom which God gives the "son of man" is eternal, invulnerable, and universal.[144] What other kingdom could the verse be referring to except God's very own Kingdom above all kingdoms? The fact that it is eternal already implies that it is God's (as opposed to the Romans' or

---

[140] John Dominic Crossan, *The Historical Jesus: The Life of a Mediterranean Jewish Peasant* (Harper Collins e-books, 2010), 6,026 of 12,350, Kindle edition; Burkett, *The Son of Man Debate*, 33.

[141] Macho, "La Cristología del Hijo del Hombre," 194.

[142] Some scholars have put forth that the sayings in which Jesus refers to himself in the third person were originally created by the early church and later put on Jesus' lips (Burkett, *The Son of Man Debate*, 56). However, the saying in Mark 13:32, in particular, is highly unlikely to have been a creation of the early church, given that it meets the criterion of embarrassment.

[143] *NLT Parallel Study Bible*, 1,550.

[144] Daniel 7:14.

Greeks'), for "only a kingdom whose authority and power are from God" "shall not be destroyed."[145] The last part of Daniel 7:14 states the following: "his dominion is an everlasting dominion, which shall not pass away, and his kingdom one that shall not be destroyed." This is echoed several times in Daniel when God is being praised by Babylonian and Persian kings:

> His kingdom is an everlasting kingdom, and his dominion endures from generation to generation.[146]
> [H]is dominion is an everlasting dominion, and his kingdom endures from generation to generation.[147]
> [F]or he is the living God, enduring forever; his kingdom shall never be destroyed, and his dominion shall be to the end.[148]

It can thus be inferred that the kingdom that the "son of man" receives and God's kingdom are one and the same. Since the "son of man" is the king of God's kingdom and his rule lasts forever, he must be the Messiah.

In Mark 14:62, Jesus most clearly points out that that it is a Messianic title, for Jesus equates the "Son of Man" with Psalm 110's "Lord" (interpreted by Jesus as the Messiah). The title is Messianic as indicated by the other sayings as well.[149] Although all of Jesus' sayings are considered significant for

---

[145] *NLT Parallel Study Bible*, 1,538.
[146] Daniel 4:3.
[147] Daniel 4:34
[148] Daniel 6:26.
[149] Bowman and Komoszewski, *Putting Jesus in His Place*, 2,766 of 4,522.

Christians, the title of Son of Man is used exclusively in sayings with the utmost significance, which are particularly associated with Jesus' "Messianic role."[150] For instance, Jesus did not say, "Have you anything here to eat,[151] for the Son of Man is hungry?"[152] Therefore, because of his "restricted usage," one can argue that Jesus was not indiscriminately exchanging the pronoun "I" with "Son of Man," even though they both have the same referent.[153]

    Daniel 7:13-14 only mentions that the Danielic figure receives authority ("dominion"), but Jesus pointed out what that authority included specifically. Mark 2:10 states that "the Son of Man has authority to forgive sins," a right which usually only belongs to God. At most the statement could be a statement referring to both the Son of Man and his disciples. But Jesus' disciples could exercise this authority only if Jesus *gave* it to them and not on their *own* authority.[154] Jesus gave the Twelve authority to cast out demons, but the disciples did it in the authority of the name of Jesus,[155] while Jesus cast them out in his own name as the Messiah, even though that authority was given to him by the Father.[156] In John 20:22-23 the disciples receive the authority to forgive sins, but only after Jesus imparts them with the Holy Spirit:

---

[150] Bowman and Komoszewski, *Putting Jesus in His Place*, 2,766 of 4,522.
[151] Luke 24:41 (Only "Have you anything here to eat" is part of verse 41 of Luke 24).
[152] Idea from Colani, *Jésus-Christ et les Croyances Messianiques de Son Temps*, 117.
[153] Burkett, *The Son of Man Debate*, 84; Colani, *Jésus-Christ et les Croyances Messianiques de Son Temps*, 117.
[154] Bowman and Komoszewski, *Putting Jesus in His Place*, 2,190-2,230 of 4,522.
[155] E.g., Mark 9:38 and 16:17.
[156] Bowman and Komoszewski, *Putting Jesus in His Place*, 2,216 of 4,522.

"he breathed on them and said to them, 'Receive the Holy Spirit. If you forgive the sins of any, they are forgiven them; if you withhold forgiveness from any, it is withheld." Likewise, the disciples, when given authority, would have perhaps had the right to forgive sins in Jesus' name, while Jesus exercised the right in his own name. Jesus demonstrated it by healing in his own name ("*I* say to you, rise, pick up your bed, and go home."[157]).[158] By contrast, the Apostle Peter for instance healed a man born lame in Jesus Christ' name: "In the name of Jesus Christ of Nazareth, rise up and walk!"[159]

    Jesus, by affirming that the Son of Man has authority over the Sabbath in Mark 2:28, rather than providing a justification for a universal breach of the Sabbath, may have instead provided a "justification for a *messianic* abrogation of the Sabbath."[160] The adverb "so" in 2:28 may have been the concluding argument not only to the statement in 2:27, but also to his example in 2:25-26, in which Jesus compares himself to David, who was not just any man, but Israel's king. Jesus was alluding to the passage in 1 Samuel 21 in which David, although not yet king, had already been chosen to be king and had been anointed by the prophet Samuel in 1 Samuel 16:13, thereby making him a type of messiah.[161]

    Jesus could have therefore meant the following in his response to the Pharisees: "If David, the one chosen by God to be king of Israel, had the right to break a law to assuage hunger, how much more the Son of Man, chosen by God to

---

[157] Mark 2:11 (italics added).
[158] Martin, "It's My Prerogative," 72.
[159] Acts 3:6.
[160] Boyarin, *The Jewish Gospels*, 68.
[161] Ibid., 67-68.

be the king of 'all nations and peoples.'¹⁶² Specifically, the divine commandment to keep the Sabbath was introduced by God to *benefit* humankind; humankind was not created for the Sabbath's sake. It follows that observing the divine command to keep the Sabbath is of less importance than safeguarding human life.¹⁶³ Accordingly, the Son of Man has the right to breach (or allow others to breach) even the Sabbath in order to assuage hunger.¹⁶⁴ In view of that, the Son of Man, the Lord over all humankind, is thus Lord of the Sabbath as well."¹⁶⁵

The religious leaders asked Jesus—not his disciples—why they were doing such things on the Sabbath, implying that as their Rabbi, Jesus should not have allowed them.¹⁶⁶ Jesus essentially meant in his response was that, as Lord of the Sabbath, he had the right to determine what could or

---

¹⁶² Daniel 7:14; Boyarin, *The Jewish Gospels*, 67-68.
¹⁶³ Cf. R. Ishmael: "How much more should the duty of saving life supersede the Sabbath laws!" ("Tractate *Shabbatta*," in *Mekilta de-Rabbi Ishmael*, Volume Three, by Jacob Z. Lauterbach (Pennsylvania: The Jewish Publication Society of America, 1935), 198). The word for "saving" is also translated as "safeguarding" (Vermes, *Jesus the Jew*, 181).
¹⁶⁴ Albert Nolan, *Jesus Before Christianity* (New York: Orbis Books, 1992), 86.
¹⁶⁵ *NLT Parallel Study Bible*, 1,768; See Exell and Spence-Jones, *The Complete Pulpit Commentary. Volume 7. Matthew to John. A Exposition, Homiletics, and Homilies Commentary on the Bible*, 63,718 and 64,238-64,252 of 161,039; Witherington, *The Gospel of Mark*, 1,967 of 7,980. Boyarin states that "one objection could be that the Sabbath is not 'under the heavens' but in heaven and thus not susceptible to the transfer of authority from the Ancient of Days to the one like a son of man. This objection is entirely answered by the statement that the Sabbath was made for the human being; consequently the Son of Man, having been given dominion in the human realm, is Lord of the Sabbath" (*The Jewish Gospels*, 67-68).
¹⁶⁶ Lindars, *Jesus Son of Man*, 102.

could not be done on that day. So just as followers of Jesus can only have the authority that is *given* to them, people can only breach the Sabbath in the circumstances *allowed* by the Son of Man, which would include doing good, saving lives, and providing for people's needs. As a result, "the Sabbath was indeed made for human beings, but only one human being, the Son of Man, was lord over the Sabbath."[167]

In Mark 8:31, the "Son of Man is linked closely with Peter's confession of Jesus as the Christ and confirms its messianic significance."[168] *Immediately* after Peter's confession concerning Jesus' Messiahship, Jesus for the first time starts making the Passion predictions about the Son of Man. Jesus was quick to point out that although he was the Messiah, contrary to expectations he was one who would have to endure suffering.[169] Six Son of Man sayings are under the "Passion" theme, but three of them simultaneously include the Son of Man's suffering, death, and resurrection. With regards to the Son of Man's suffering, Jesus was probably alluding to the account of the "Suffering Servant," a passage that Jesus undoubtedly interpreted as Messianic. Jesus' prophecy about his death also alluded perhaps to Daniel 9:26,[170] in which it is stated that "an anointed one shall be cut off and shall have nothing."[171] This passage could thus be held as a prophecy about the coming Messiah's death. The

---

[167] Witherington, *The Gospel of Mark*, 1,992 of 7,980.
[168] *NLT Parallel Study Bible*, 1,847.
[169] Witherington, *The Christology of Jesus*, 261.
[170] Albert Barnes, "Commentary on Matthew 26:4," "Barnes' Notes on the New Testament," *StudyLight.org*, last accessed April 22, 2019, https://www.studylight.org/commentaries/bnb/matthew-26.html, 1870; Rowe, "Is Daniel's 'Son of Man' Messianic?" 93.
[171] *NLT Parallel Study Bible*, 1,782.

additional allusion to Isaiah 53 would have been necessary to explain the *purpose* of the Son of Man's death.[172]

The resurrection is *the* central miracle of Christianity, and the chief one among his "rule miracles" (that show Jesus' authority).[173] One of the purposes of the resurrection was to demonstrate his authority, as indirectly indicated in Mark, and more explicitly in John. When asked on what authority he was driving out the merchants and money-changers out of the Temple, Jesus answered, "Destroy this temple, and in three days I will raise it up."[174] This saying is first echoed in Mark 14:58, in which witnesses say concerning Jesus, "We heard him say, 'I will destroy this temple that is made with hands, and in three days I will build another, not made with hands.'" Then again in Mark 15:29-30: "Aha! You who would destroy the temple and rebuild it in three days, save yourself, and come down from the cross!" It would not be unreasonable to assume that Jesus meant that the miracle would have proven his authority as the Messiah, not just as a prophet.

Mark 10:45 also has strong Messianic connotations, for Jesus was saying that the Son of Man's death was not just the death of any martyr, but was a death that would provide atonement from sins. The hope for a Messiah may have been prevalent in the 1st century CE, but this constituted a notion profoundly opposite to the religious sentiments of the Jews at the time, who were expecting a conquering Davidic king.[175] Instead of a conquering Messiah that delivered the Gentiles (i.e., the Romans) into Israel's hands, Jesus introduced

---

[172] Jeremias, *New Testament Theology*, 286-288.
[173] Bock, *Studying the Historical Jesus*, 3,716 of 4,412.
[174] John 2:19.
[175] Colani, *Jésus-Christ et les Croyances Messianiques de Son Temps*, 131 ; 138; Horbury, *Jewish Messianism and the Cult of Christ*, 112.

himself as the Messiah who would be (temporarily) delivered into the Gentiles' hands.[176] And paradoxically, his death would bring life to others.

In Mark 9:12, it was even known by the disciples that Elijah was to "come first," that is, before the Messiah. Jesus confirmed it, and then in the next sentence in the verse he used the title of Son of Man. Moreover, Mark 8:38 and 13:26-27 implicitly describe the Son of Man as the judge of humanity (made explicit in the other Gospels), which is also a role reserved for God alone.

2. Jesus' Use of a Messianic Title That Was Unknown and Ambiguous

If Jesus used it as a Messianic title, it does not mean that others would have recognized it as such. It is curious that in Mark, Jesus generally employs the title when addressing only the Twelve or the religious leaders.[177] There are crowds present at times when using the term (as in Mark 2:10 and 14:62), but in preaching to the crowds Jesus focused mainly on the kingdom of God.[178] Only in Mark 8:38 does Jesus refer to the Son of Man when addressing the crowds (in addition to his disciples).[179] In Mark, not only is Jesus never criticized nor accused of blasphemy for using the title, Jesus receives no reactions at all—either positive or negative—

---

[176] Colani, *Jésus-Christ et les Croyances Messianiques de Son Temps*, 130.

[177] Witherington, *The Gospel of Mark*, 4,298 of 7,980.

[178] Jeremias, *New Testament Theology*, 267-268.

[179] Ibid. In the Gospels, the Son of Man sayings and the sayings about the kingdom of God almost never occur simultaneously, but according to Jeremias, this can be explained by the fact that Jesus would preach to the public generally about the kingdom of God (in the form of parables), but he would specifically refer to the Son of Man—the King of God's kingdom—when speaking only to his disciples (or when answering the religious authorities) (Ibid.).

from either his disciples or the Jewish leaders when voicing the title.[180]

Furthermore, when Jesus asks his disciples who people think he is, they respond with several opinions people had concerning his identity:[181] "John the Baptist; and others say, Elijah; and others, one of the prophets."[182] Also, in addition to the Messiah, people were waiting for the Son of David (another Messianic title) as implied in Mark 12:35, but made explicit in Matthew 12:23: "And all the people were amazed, and said, 'Can this be the Son of David?'" Yet the Son of Man seems not to have been any of the options.[183] The only exceptions come from the Gospel of John, where in 12:34 some in the crowd seem to link Messiah and Son of Man together, but at the same time they seem confused because "the Son of Man must be lifted up," yet they "heard from the Law that the Christ remains forever."[184] Similarly, in John 9:35-38, the man who was healed from blindness seems to understand it as a Messianic title as well, although he did not know Jesus was referring to himself.[185] Jesus may or may not have created the Messianic title, depending mainly on whether *Similitudes*—which uses the designation in a titular or quasi-titular manner—is pre-Christian. What seems clear, however, is that it was never commonly used as a Messianic

---

[180] Nolan, *Jesus Before Christianity*, 145; Vermes, *Jesus the Jew*, 161.
[181] Larry W. Hurtado, "Summary and Concluding Observations," in *'Who is This Son of Man?': The Latest Scholarship on a Puzzling Expression of the Historical Jesus*, ed. Larry W. Hurtado and Paul L. Owen et al. (New York: Bloomsbury T & T Clark, 2011), 163.
[182] Mark 8:28.
[183] Hurtado, "Summary and Concluding Observations," 163.
[184] John 12:34; Reynolds, "The Use of the Son of Man Idiom in the Gospel of John," 110.
[185] Ibid., 118.

title (especially when compared to the title of "Messiah"), and, at least judging from the evidence within and without the New Testament, it was generally not a title people would recognize as a Messianic title either.[186]

Why then, would Jesus make a Messianic title out of such a recondite expression? Why not just call himself "the Messiah"? There are two major reasons as to why Jesus may have avoided using the title "Messiah": (1) due to the preconceived notions that lay behind the title of "the Messiah," for the Messiah was expected to be a political Davidic king who would deliver the Israelites from the oppression of the Romans;[187] (2) So as to not spark excessive controversy so early in his ministry, while simultaneously declaring himself the Messiah in a veiled manner.[188]

When speaking solely to the Twelve, Jesus may have avoided using "the Messiah" as a title in order "to avoid the nationalistic and political ideas that the people associated with" the title.[189] Plus, the title of Messiah as popularly understood did not carry the connotations of suffering that the title had to have.[190] By choosing to use the title of Son of Man, Jesus was pouring new wine (an unexpected Messianic

---

[186] Burkett, *The Son of Man Debate*, 69; Collins, *The Scepter and the Star*, 193.
[187] Burkett, *The Son of Man Debate*, 69.
[188] Ibid.; Cf. D. A. Carson, "Matthew" in *The Expositor's Bible Commentary*, Volume 8, ed. Frank E. Gaebelein (Michigan: Zondervan Pub. House, 1984), 212-213.
[189] Burkett, *The Son of Man Debate*, 69.
[190] Bock, "The Use of Daniel 7 in Jesus' Trial," 83; Norman Perrin, "Son of Man in the Synoptic tradition," *Biblical Research* 13, (January 1, 1968): 20-21, last accessed October 20, 2013, ATLA Religion Database with ATLASerials, EBSCOhost.

concept) into a new wineskin (new title).[191] Once his disciples understood the nature of his Messiahship following his resurrection, the proper time came for his disciples to proclaim him as the Messiah, starting with Jesus himself. Following his resurrection, Jesus no longer used the title of the Son of Man again, but did call himself "Christ" twice (in Luke 24:26 and 24:46) and "Son" once (in Matthew 28:19). Jesus even used "Christ" in a saying that would lend itself to using the title of Son of Man, a saying in which he was telling his disciples what was prophesized in Scriptures: "Thus it is written, that the Christ should suffer and on the third day rise from the dead."[192]

When addressing the religious leaders, the title of the Son of Man revealed his identity as the Messiah, yet because it was a largely unknown title, Jesus delayed additional or more severe clashes with the religious teachers from breaking out. In the initial clash recorded in Mark 2:1-12, after the religious leaders are offended, Jesus responds with the reference to the Son of Man.[193] He responds likewise in the Sabbath controversy of 2:23-28. By using the title, Jesus thus provided the leaders and teachers with an explanation (albeit oblique one) as to who he was and why he had authority to do what he did: simply because he is the Messiah. The circumlocutory title possibly enabled Jesus to declare his

---

[191] Idea from F. F. Bruce, "The Background to the Son of Man sayings," in *Christ the Lord*, ed. Harold H. Rowdon (Leicester, UK: Inter-Varsity Press, 1982), 70.
[192] Luke 24:46.
[193] Bowman and Komoszewski, *Putting Jesus in His Place*, 2,707 of 4,522.

Messiahship and make claims about himself, but in an oblique manner.[194]

Jesus meant it as a Messianic title, but others may have *understood* the Son of Man as a merely circumlocutional idiom or as a generic expression (at least initially), as some scholars still do today.[195] Jesus may have deliberately made use of the inherent ambiguity of the designation,[196] for a saying like in Mark 2:28 may have at first *seemed* like a generic or indefinite statement about man in general or any man being lord over the Sabbath, but upon closer inspection, especially when taking into account the saying's historical and narrative context, one realizes that it can only hold true for Jesus. That many may have misunderstood it as a nontitular idiom would in turn explain why there was no reaction to his use of the title, for not only was it not a well-known title, it was perhaps not interpreted as one at times. Precisely because Mark 2:10 and 2:28 sound generic, his Messianic claims may have not registered immediately for some.

Even his disciples were at odds at what he meant at times. For instance, after Jesus predicts that he would be "delivered into the hands of men," "killed," and then resurrected "after three days" in a Son of Man saying in Mark 9:31, Mark 9:32 states: "But they did not understand the saying, and were afraid to ask him." The Apostles perhaps did not realize until afterwards that the Son of Man was a title.

3. The Early Church's Use of the Title and of the Book of Daniel

---

[194] Cf. Barnabas Lindars, "Re-Enter the Apocalyptic Son of Man," *New Testament Studies* 21, no. 1 (October, 1975), 71; Carson, "Matthew," 212.
[195] Carson, "Matthew," 212-213.
[196] Ibid., 212.

Nevertheless, some scholars argue that the early Christian community reinterpreted what would have only originally been an idiomatic expression by combining it with the Danielic "son of man" and making it a Messianic title.[197] Although Daniel 7:13 is explicitly quoted only once in Mark (in 14:62), it has been shown that Daniel is not only the basis for the title of the Son of Man, but that Daniel's thematic and prophetic content is also most probably the basis for the Son of Man sayings themselves. Thus if Jesus merely had used a nontitular idiom which the early church subsequently linked to Daniel 7, one would have to view most—if not all—of the Son of Man sayings from the Gospel of Mark—generally considered the earliest written account of Jesus' life—as inauthentic because the book of Daniel is at least implicitly a basis for them.[198] Furthermore, it would have been unlikely for early Christians to have gone through the trouble of making the connection to the apocalyptic book of Daniel subtle enough that the interpretation that it was a Messianic title derived from Daniel did not become prevalent until the 19th century CE.[199] As Darrell Bock asks, "Would a post-Easter creation be so subtle?"[200]

As presented in the previous chapter, both the use of "Son of Man" and the allusions to Daniel were distinctive of

---

[197] Geza Vermes, *The Changing Faces of Jesus* (New York: Penguin Books, 2000), 189. Casey also argues that it was an idiomatic expression which was later made into "a major new Christological title," which was "just what the church needed" (Casey, *The Solution to the 'Son of Man' Problem*, 4,378 of 6,420).

[198] Vermes, *Jesus the Jew*, 184; Witherington, *The Christology of Jesus*, 256-257.

[199] Burkett, *The Son of Man Debate*, 24.

[200] Bock, "The Use of Daniel 7 in Jesus' Trial," 83. Bock asks this question regarding Mark 12:35-37, but it may also be asked concerning the title of Son of Man.

Jesus. The Epistles never quote Daniel at all nor refer to Jesus as "the Son of Man," and apart from the ones Jesus makes, the only allusions to Daniel 7 in the New Testament—which are in the book of Revelation—are simply part of a vision in which Jesus is identified as the Danielic "son of man."[201] Perhaps the earliest Christians did not use the title because they did not interpret the Son of Man as a title. However, it is more likely that the early church interpreted it as a title (yet had no need to use it), given that starting with the first known interpretation in 108 CE, Christians continually interpreted the expression as a title (although not necessarily one derived from Daniel 7:13). It was not until the 16th century that the interpretation that it was a nontitular idiom was postulated.[202]

Moreover, further evidence suggests that the pillars of the church—not only the evangelists—were aware of Jesus' Son of Man sayings, but had no *need* to either use the title or to reference the book of Daniel. When mentioning Jesus' future coming in the Letter of 1 Thessalonians (one of the earliest undisputed ones of the Apostle Paul written around 51 CE),[203] Paul seems to be echoing a saying in Mark in which Jesus himself is alluding to Daniel 7:13:[204]

> For this we declare to you by a word from the Lord, that we who are alive, who are left until the coming of the Lord, will not precede those who have fallen asleep. For the Lord himself will descend from heaven with a cry of command, with the voice of an archangel,

---

[201] Crossan, *The Historical Jesus*, 5,824 of 12,350.
[202] Burkett, *The Son of Man Debate*, 83.
[203] *NLT Parallel Study Bible*, 2,267.
[204] Collins and Collins, *King and Messiah as Son of God*, 171-172.

and with the sound of the trumpet of God. And the dead in Christ will rise first. Then we who are alive, who are left, will be caught up together with them in the clouds to meet the Lord in the air, and so we will always be with the Lord.[205]

Paul seems to be echoing the saying of Jesus in Mark 13:26-27.[206] The Letter shows that the Apostle Paul may have been aware of a Son of Man saying alluding to Daniel 7 as early as the 50s CE. Paul most probably understood the Son of Man to be a title, for, according to the book of Acts, he was a witness to the expression being used as a title by Stephen in 7:56: "Behold, I see the heavens opened, and the Son of Man standing at the right hand of God." The book of Acts shows that Paul would have been aware of the Son of Man title early on, before he even became Christian. Consequently, Paul referred to the return of Jesus without needing either to use the title or to refer to Daniel.[207]

The same can be said concerning the following passage in 2 Peter, although it is a disputed Letter and was written around 67 CE:[208] "For we did not follow cleverly devised myths when we made known to you the power and coming of our Lord Jesus Christ, but we were eyewitnesses of his majesty."[209] The verse seems to be echoing Mark 8:31 or Mark 13:26-27, indicating that Peter may have been aware of at least of one Son of Man saying which alluded to Daniel 7,

---

[205] 1 Thessalonians 4:15-17.
[206] Collins and Collins, *King and Messiah as Son of God*, 171-172.
[207] Crossan, *The Historical Jesus*, 5,774 of 12,350.
[208] *NLT Parallel Study Bible*, 2,377.
[209] 2 Peter 1: 16.

while at the same time not using the title (most probably because he did not need to), nor needing to quote Daniel.

Furthermore, the non-canonical but early writing of *Didache*, written in late first century or early second century CE[210] (though not by one of the Apostles), frequently alludes to Jesus' sayings, including one of his sayings in 16:8, in which Jesus himself is referring to Daniel 7:13: "Then the world will see the Lord coming atop the clouds of heaven,"[211] probably also alluding to Mark 13:26.[212] The author of *Didache* again made no reference to the book of Daniel. The author wrote "Lord" instead of "the Son of Man" probably because he preferred the former title. If the author did not read the Son of Man as a title, it would only reinforce the view that the title truly came from Jesus.

An alternative explanation to the fact that the Epistles do not refer to Jesus as the "Son of Man," nor to the book of Daniel, may be that the Epistles were addressed to communities that were already preached to, meaning that they would have already have received the explanation of how Jesus was the Messiah on the basis of Daniel.[213] Yet the book of Romans, Paul's longest Letter in the Bible, was addressed to a community which Paul had not yet met.[214] The Letter does not quote the book of Daniel at all either. Also, in Peter's preaching in Acts 2:14-40, in which he is publicly declaring Jesus as the Messiah for the first time on the day of

---

[210] Bowman and Komoszewski, *Putting Jesus in His Place*, 3,411 of 4,522.
[211] Aaron Milavec, trans., *The Didache: Text, Translation, Analysis, and Commentary* (Minnesota: Liturgical Press, 2003), 37.
[212] Crossan, *The Historical Jesus*, 5,792 of 12,350.
[213] Idea of alternative explanation from Collins and Collins, *King and Messiah as Son of God*, 116.
[214] Collins and Collins, *King and Messiah as Son of God*, 116.

Pentecost, in front of a large Jewish audience, Peter never refers to Jesus as the "Son of Man," nor to the book of Daniel. Yet Peter does allude to Joel 2:28-32, Psalm 16:8-11, and Psalm 110:1.[215]

Proceeding on the reasonable assumption that the 1st century CE Christians interpreted the Son of Man as a title (as from the earliest interpretation in the 2nd century CE onwards, the expression was interpreted as a title), the earliest Christians probably did not use the title, despite being a Messianic title, because they simply did not *need* it. It did not suit their proselytizing purposes to use a title so abstruse and unrecognizable, which only meant "the human being" in idiomatic Aramaic.[216] The early church was anything but subtle in proclaiming Jesus as the Messiah, therefore using the ambiguous title would not have been consistent with their clear-cut preaching. Even today, it is highly unlikely that a Christian, whether "preaching to the choir" or proselytizing, will refer to Jesus as "the Son of Man." As was the case for Jesus' Apostles, Christians today are far more likely to refer to Jesus as "Christ" or "the Son of God."

Statistics corroborate the view that the early church had no need for the title (again assuming they also saw the expression as a title), much preferring other Christological titles that were unambiguous. Excluding the number of times the titles appear on Jesus' lips, the authors of the New Testament books mention "the Christ" (or "the Messiah") 43 times, "the Son of God" 37 times, but "the Son of Man" only 4 times.[217] Evidently for the New Testament authors, "the

---

[215] *The Holy Bible, New International Version* (Michigan: Zondervan, 2011), 992-993.
[216] Burkett, *The Son of Man Debate*, 63; cf. Boyarin, *The Jewish Gospels*, 36.
[217] *Accordance*.

Christ" (or "the Messiah") is the preferred title used in reference to Jesus out of the three, being mentioned 51.1% of the time. Jesus himself uses "the Son of Man" more than the other two titles (85.9% of his use of these three titles are to Son of Man). Thus, Jesus prefers the title that the authors of the New Testament themselves ignore the most; only 4.8% of the titles used for Jesus by these authors are Son of Man (excluding the occasions when they report Jesus using it). The comparative usage of the three Christological titles throughout the New Testament is shown in the following graph:[218]

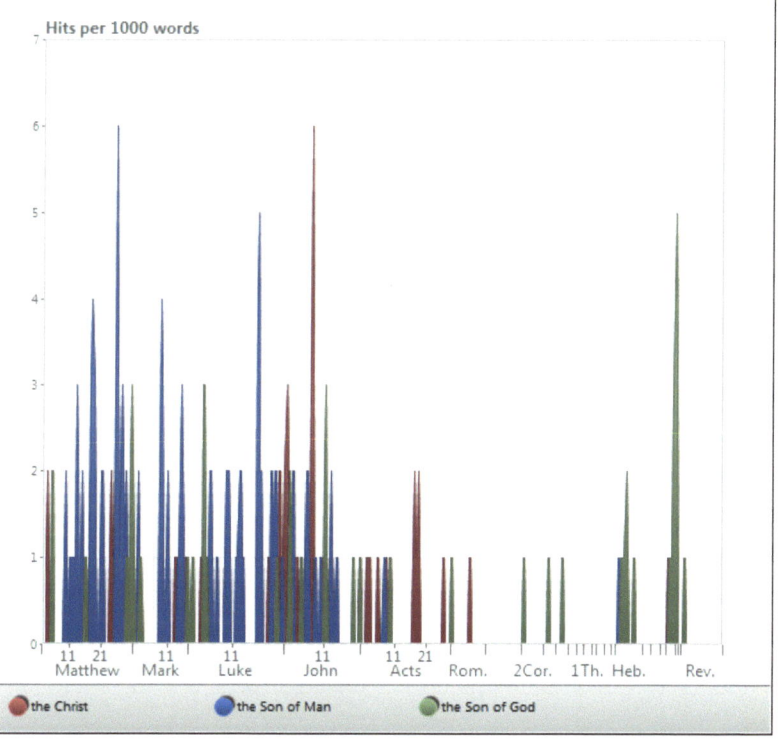

---

[218] Adapted from *Accordance*.

Virtually all of the blue represents the instances in which Jesus pronounces the title (95.2%). Of all the references to "the Christ," the vast majority (84.3%) are not uttered by Jesus. Similarly, among all the references to "the Son of God," 90.2% are not uttered by Jesus.

Given that "Christ" often appears as a last name for Jesus in the New Testament, the contrast becomes even more apparent when comparing, in particular, the usage of "Christ" without the definite article to that of "Son of Man," also without the definite article:[219]

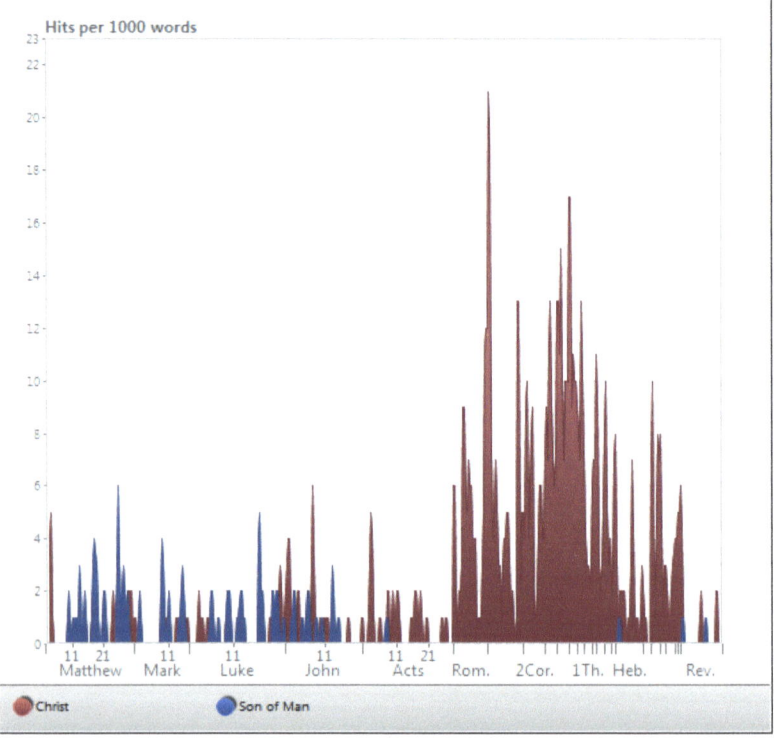

---

[219] Graph adapted from *Accordance*. I am assuming that the appellation of "Christ" in "Jesus Christ" was not meant as a mere last name, but also as a title for Jesus.

Again, the vast majority of the blue represents the instances in which Jesus pronounces the title (96.3%), while Christian authors use nearly all of the occurrences of "Christ" (97.8%) which are not included in Jesus' words. The graph confirms the view that the ambiguous title of Son of Man would have not been useful to an early church that was already profusely using the unequivocal title of Christ.

In the Gospels, the title of Son of Man is never used outside of speech (whether direct or indirect), and occurs nearly every time in Jesus' sayings. This again suggests that the evangelists were recording the title of Son of Man because they were faithfully preserving the Son of Man sayings, not because they necessarily needed or preferred the title itself. In the Gospel of Mark, the evangelist's preference for the Christological titles of Messiah (or Christ) and Son of God over Son of Man is suggested in the Gospel's very first verse: "The beginning of the gospel of Jesus Christ, the Son of God."[220] Despite being a Messianic title, the Son of Man was not included by the evangelist with the other Christological titles that were by far the most used by the early Christians. If the evangelist needed the title of Son of Man, the first verse would have provided an excellent opportunity for him to have included it. In the unlikely event that the evangelist—or any author of the New Testament—only interpreted the title as a nontitular idiom (which would provide an alternative explanation as to why it was not used), it would only confirm the view that the Messianic title truly came from Jesus.

As time went on, the early Christian community had increasingly *less* of a reason to use the Son of Man because

---

[220] Mark 1:1.

Greek-speaking Gentiles, who would have known nothing about the *Tanakh* or Aramaic, became a more and more a prominent segment of Christians over the years. The title of "the Son of God" *would*, however, have probably been understood when preaching to the Gentiles, given that, for instance, the Roman Emperor Augustus was divinized by being called *divi filius* (i.e., Son of God); therefore the Gentiles of the Roman Empire would have most probably understood "Son of God" as a claim to divinity.[221]

The early church was explicitly proclaiming the Messiahship that Jesus himself was implicitly signaling.[222] As Evans states, "Jesus did indeed understand himself as Israel's Messiah. The messianic identity of Jesus is no post-Easter Christian invention."[223]

---

[221] Collins and Collins, *King and Messiah as Son of God*, 53.
[222] Leonardo Boff, *Jesus Christ Liberator: A Critical Christology for Our Time*, trans. Patrick Hughes (New York: Orbis Books, 1978), 13.
[223] Evans, *Fabricating Jesus*, 46.

IV. THE SON OF MAN AS DIVINE MESSIAH
A. The Divine Messiah

"The Son of Man" was probably not used merely to avoid being identified as the type of Messiah he was not, but to *affirm* the type of Messiah Jesus was. Although Jesus accepted titles such as "Messiah," "Son of David," "Rabbi," and "Prophet," none of them may have fully described the role he had.[1] In the final clash with the Jewish leaders in 14:53-65, when the time came to most unambiguously reveal his identity, Jesus still referred to himself as "the Son of Man."[2] Jesus may have thus used this title not only to contrast with the expected Davidic Messiah or reveal his identity in an oblique manner, but also to indicate an even more glorious Messiah.[3] The Danielic figure behind the title seems not only to be a heavenly Messiah ("with the clouds of heaven") with universal rule, but a divine one as well.[4]

1. The Heavenly "Son of Man" from Daniel

The words "with the clouds of heaven" not only indicate that the Messianic figure is a heavenly one—in complete contrast to the beasts coming out of the sea in the same vision—but may also be suggesting that he is divine in

---

[1] Timothée Colani, *Jésus-Christ et les Croyances Messianiques de Son Temps* (Strasbourg, France: Treuttel Et Wurtz, Librairies- Editeurs, 1864), 114.

[2] Robert M. Bowman Jr. and J. Ed Komoszewski, *Putting Jesus in His Place: The Case for the Deity of Christ* (Michigan: Kregel Publications, 2007), 2,707 of 4,522, Kindle edition; D. A. Carson, "Matthew" in *The Expositor's Bible Commentary*, Volume 8, ed. Frank E. Gaebelein (Michigan: Zondervan Pub. House, 1984), 213.

[3] Cf. Bowman and Komoszewski, *Putting Jesus in His Place*, 2,713 and 2,729 of 4,522.

[4] Bowman and Komoszewski, *Putting Jesus in His Place*, 2,763 of 4,522.

some sense.[5] Although the mention of "clouds of heaven" may only be indicating that the scene takes place "above," there is evidence from the Bible to suggest that the symbolic clouds are numinous ones pointing to the Messiah's divinity.[6] Throughout the *Tanakh*, clouds often point to God's Presence or Glory.[7] In Daniel they may be at least indirectly linked with the Glory of God, for the "son of man" receives "glory" from God in 7:14. In the ESV, out of the 132 occurrences of "cloud(s)" in the *Tanakh*, roughly half of them point to God's Presence and/or Glory (the other half mostly refer to actual clouds of nature).[8] However, there are only nine verses in the *Tanakh* which include both "cloud" (or "clouds") and a conjugated form of the verb "to come."[9] The

---

[5] *NLT Parallel Study Bible* (Illinois: Tyndale House Publishers, Inc., 2011), 1,550; José Ramón Scheifler, "El Hijo del Hombre en Daniel," *Estudios Eclesiásticos* 34, no. 134-135 (July 1, 1960): 803, last accessed January 22, 2014, ATLA Religion Database with ATLASerials, EBSCOhost.

[6] Bowman and Komoszewski, *Putting Jesus in His Place*, 2,765-2,766 of 4,522; Daniel Boyarin, *The Jewish Gospels: The Story of the Jewish Christ* (New York: The New Press, 2012 (the paperback edition I used was published in 2013)), 39-40, 44; Ben Witherington, III, *The Gospel of Mark: A Socio-Rhetorical Commentary* (Michigan and Cambridge, UK: Wm. B. Eerdmans Publishing Company, 2001), 3,904 of 7,980, Kindle edition.

[7] Louis F. Hartman and Alexander A. Di Lella, *The Book of Daniel*, trans. Louis F. Hartman, The Anchor Bible (New York: Doubleday, 1978), 101; Boyarin, *The Jewish Gospels*, 39-40; *NLT Parallel Study Bible*, 1,550.

[8] *Accordance.*

[9] Ibid. In Biblical Hebrew there are three different verbs underlying what the ESV renders as a form of the verb "to come" in the verses: בוא (to "come"); ירד (to "come down"); קרב (to "come near"); and עלה (to "go up"). Daniel 7:13 uses the Aramaic verb אתה (to "come") (William L. Holladay, ed., *A Concise Hebrew and Aramaic Lexicon of the Old Testament* (Michigan: Wm. B. Eerdmans Publishing Co., 1988), 34, 143, 27, 324, 398).

verses are the following: Exodus 19:9; Numbers 11:25 and 12:5; Deuteronomy 4:11; Jeremiah 4:13; Ezekiel 1:4, 38:9, and 38:16; and Daniel 7:13. The first five of them point to God's Presence and Glory. Jeremiah 4:13 and Ezekiel 1:4 are linked specifically with God's judgment,[10] either pointing to God (who judges directly) or to kings or nations whom God uses as instruments for judgment. The verses Ezekiel 38:9 and 38:16 may be two exceptions, for although they occur in the context of judgment, they refer to Gog coming "like a cloud",[11] and God does not carry out judgment through that nation, but on the nation of Gog. Nevertheless, most of the verses can be linked with "God's Presence"—the *Shekinah*—for the verses pointing to God's Glory and judgment both signal God's Presence.[12] Jesus precisely associated God's Glory and Judgment in his Son of Man sayings in the Gospels, with an example in Mark being in 13:26-7: "And then they will see the Son of Man coming in clouds with great power and glory. And then he will send out the angels and gather his elect from the four winds, from the ends of the earth to the ends of heaven."[13] The other Markan verses under the theme of exaltation (8:38 and 14:62) also associate the Son of Man with God's Glory.

---

[10] The word "judgment" is written with a lowercase "j" in order to differentiate a judgment of God (among many) from God's final Judgment.
[11] Ezekiel 38:16.
[12] Bowman and Komoszewski, *Putting Jesus in His Place*, 1,231 of 4,522.
[13] Benjamin E. Reynolds, "The Use of the Son of Man Idiom in the Gospel of John," in *'Who is This Son of Man?': The Latest Scholarship on a Puzzling Expression of the Historical Jesus*, ed. Larry W. Hurtado and Paul L. Owen et al. (New York: Bloomsbury T & T Clark, 2011), 126.

The Danielic figure is also one that everyone "should serve."[14] The Aramaic verb behind the word "serve" from Daniel 7:14 is פלח (*pelach*).[15] In Daniel, this Aramaic verb (conjugated in different forms) further occurs in 3:12, 14, 17, 18, 28; 6:16, 20; and 7:27.[16] In extra-Biblical texts, such as the Targums to the Pentateuch and to Isaiah, the verb *pelach* is not only used in the context of service as to a deity, but also in reference to specific (human) individuals.[17] However, in the particular context of the book of Daniel, פלח may nevertheless be a key word in determining the identity of the "son of man."[18]

Apart from Daniel 7:14 and 7:27, in which it may be disputed as to who exactly people "should serve," the verb פלח is always used in Daniel in reference to either God or the Babylonian king's gods.[19] The verb is used in the contexts of either the refusal of "serving" other gods (3:12, 14, 18), or the affirmation of the "service" of God (3:17, 6:16, 6:20). In 3:28, both the refusal to "serve" other gods and the affirmation to "serve" God occur together: "[they] yielded up their bodies rather than serve and worship any god except their own God." Yet in the context of the book of Daniel, it is clear that Daniel and his friends do not refuse to serve the king as a human ruler, respecting the king and the law of the land (as long as it does not infringe on their worship of God). Consequently, in Daniel it seems that פלח is used, as Bowman

---

[14] Daniel 7:14.
[15] Bowman and Komoszewski, *Putting Jesus in His Place*, 643 of 4,522.
[16] Ibid., 647 of 4,522.
[17] Scheifler, "El Hijo del Hombre en Daniel," 804.
[18] Bowman and Komoszewski, *Putting Jesus in His Place*, 649 of 4,522.
[19] Ibid., 643 of 4,522.

and Komoszewski state, "to refer to rendering religious service or performing religious rituals in honor of a deity."[20]

The Babylonian king in Daniel 2:37 and 5:18 receives from God a "kingdom," "power," "might," "glory," "greatness," and "majesty." Afterwards, Nebuchadnezzar built a statue of himself and ordered everyone to worship it, but it was done on his own volition, out of his own conceit.[21] Moreover, a few administrators, jealous of Daniel, put in place a law that prohibited people from praying to anyone except king Darius the Mede. Yet it seems that in 7:14 that God *approves* of the service of the Danielic figure since in the context of the passage the authority seems to have been given by God.[22] As Bowman and Komoszewski state, "The 'service' that Daniel and his friends refused to give to Nebuchadnezzar's image or to Darius, Daniel envisions all nations giving to the heavenly Son of Man."[23] Also, since the "son of man" is to be served by "all peoples," it would of course include the Israelites. It may thus be implied that the "son of man" receives divine worship, and that God approves of the divine worship of the "son of man" by everyone, including the Israelites.

Moreover, when one takes into account that the "son of man" is (1) a heavenly being linked with God's Glory; (2) the king of God's universal and eternal kingdom; and (3) a heavenly king that would be served forever by everyone, it becomes difficult to come to any other conclusion than that the figure is divine.[24] That Jesus also probably interpreted the

---

[20] Bowman and Komoszewski, *Putting Jesus in His Place*, 643 of 4,522.
[21] *NLT Parallel Study Bible*, 1,539.
[22] Cf. Bowman and Komoszewski, *Putting Jesus in His Place*, 647 of 4,522.
[23] Bowman and Komoszewski, *Putting Jesus in His Place*, 647 of 4,522.
[24] Ibid., 649-659 and 2,769 of 4,522.

Danielic figure as divine is also implied in his Son of Man sayings.

2. The Son of Man: A Claim to Divinity

When Jesus responded "I am" in Mark 14:62, it may have simply consisted of a favorable answer to the question regarding his Messianic identity.[25] Jesus may not have even responded with "I am," but with "You have said so," as in Matthew 26:64. But given the context, Jesus may have been making a divine claim, alluding to the name God disclosed to Moses in the account of the burning bush in Exodus 3:14: "'I AM WHO I AM.' And he said, 'Say this to the people of Israel: 'I AM has sent me to you.'"[26] Jesus then combines Daniel 7:13 with Psalm 110 in his response to the Sanhedrin, a unique combination in the New Testament.[27] In the first verse of the Psalm, the Messiah is told to sit at the "right hand" of the LORD. Whether Jesus meant equality with God may be debated, but the combination of (1) Jesus' "I am" statement; (2) the Son of Man being seated at God's side; (3) and the Son of Man being associated with God's Glory ("with

---

[25] *NLT Parallel Study Bible*, 1,875.

[26] Boyarin, *The Jewish Gospels*, 138-139; *NLT Parallel Study Bible*, 1,875; Witherington, *The Gospel of Mark*, 5,767 of 7,980.

[27] Bock, "The Use of Daniel 7 in Jesus' Trial, with Implications for his Self-Understanding," in *'Who is This Son of Man?': The Latest Scholarship on a Puzzling Expression of the Historical Jesus*, ed. Larry W. Hurtado and Paul L. Owen et al. (New York: Bloomsbury T & T Clark, 2011), 95; Bowman and Komoszewski, *Putting Jesus in His Place*, 2,843 of 4,522; Barnabas Lindars, *Jesus Son of Man: A Fresh Examination of the Son of Man Sayings in the Gospels in the Light of Recent Research* (Michigan: Wm. B. Eerdmans, 1983), 110; Ben Witherington, III, *The Christology of Jesus* (Minneapolis, Minnesota: Fortress Press, 1990), 258.

the clouds of heaven there came …") cumulatively point towards the Son of Man being divine.[28]

That Jesus was claiming to be a divine Messiah is also supported by the fact that the religious authorities accused him of blasphemy.[29] In addition to claiming to be the Messiah, it seems that Jesus would have been required to have been understood as claiming equality with God to have been charged with blasphemy on legal grounds.[30] They probably understood Jesus' claim of being at God's right hand as perhaps infringing "the incommensurateness and unity of God."[31] And for the religious authorities to have regarded Jesus's answer not only as blasphemy, but one deserving the death penalty, he would have probably needed to have said the divine name as well.[32] Given the reaction from the religious leaders in Mark 14:63, perhaps they

---

[28] Bock, "The Use of Daniel 7 in Jesus' Trial," 95; Witherington, *The Gospel of Mark*, 5,764 of 7,980.

[29] Bock, "The Use of Daniel 7 in Jesus' Trial," 95-96; Bowman and Komoszewski, *Putting Jesus in His Place*, 2,769-2,774 of 4,522.

[30] Bowman and Komoszewski, *Putting Jesus in His Place*, 2,697; 2,704, and 2,771 of 4,522; Joel Marcus, "Mark 14:61: 'Are you the Messiah-Son-of-God?'" *Novum Testamentum* 31, no. 2 (April 1, 1989): 140-141, last accessed September 28, 2013, ATLA Religion Database with ATLASerials, EBSCOhost.

[31] Marcus, "Mark 14:61," 141.

[32] Craig A. Evans, *Ancient Texts for New Testament Studies: A Guide to the Background Literature* (Minneapolis, Minnesota: Baker Academic, 2005), 222: according to the *Mishnah*, that someone charged with blasphemy should be sentenced to death for pronouncing the divine name is indicated by *Sanhedrin* 7:5, on the basis of the Biblical passage of Leviticus 24:15.

interpreted Jesus' "I am" answer as uttering God's divine name from Exodus 3:14.[33]

With regards to divine prerogatives, only God has the right to forgive sins, yet the Son of Man claims precisely that same right. It is implicit in Mark that the Son of Man has the authority to judge humanity, which is also God's prerogative. In Mark 2:28, Jesus was also arguably claiming an exclusive divine right, for who else can be the Lord of a "divine institution" like the Sabbath aside from the "Divine Lord"?[34] Also, even the "elect" belong to the Son of Man.[35]

Furthermore, concerning Jesus' sacrificial death referred to in Mark 10:45, how could he possibly atone for the sins of humanity if he were a mere human?[36] The central miracle of the resurrection also implies a claim for divinity, for only God could possibly raise Himself from the dead ("Destroy this temple, and in three days *I* will raise it up."[37]).[38]

As a result, the Son of Man, who sits at God's right hand, has authority and power: to forgive sins, to judge humanity, over the Sabbath, to atone for humankind's sins, and to raise himself from the dead. Altogether, the Son of

---

[33] However, an alternative explanation is that Jesus uttered the divine name when stating the phrase "right hand of Power," but had actually said the divine name instead of "Power" (William Lane Craig, *Reasonable Faith: Christian Truth and Apologetics* (Illinois: Crossway, 2008), 318).

[34] Barton W. Johnson, "The People's New Testament," *Bible Hub*, last accessed April 26, 2019,
https://biblehub.com/commentaries/pnt/mark/2.htm; 1891; *NLT Parallel Study Bible*, 1,829.

[35] Mark 13:27.

[36] Erik Larson (class notes).

[37] John 2:19 (italics added).

[38] Bowman and Komoszewski, *Putting Jesus in His Place*, 1,192 and 2,567 of 4,522.

Man's job description implies that Jesus was indeed claiming to be God when using that title.[39]

One therefore arrives at a paradox brought about by Jesus in a manner that was characteristic of him: Jesus chose an expression that meant simply "the human being" in Aramaic and made it into a title indicating his divinity.[40] Out of all the Christological titles, it seems like the most insignificant one and yet the one that arguably emphasizes his divinity the most.[41] Jesus' following aphorism could thus be applied to the title: "But many who are first will be last, and the last first."[42] The Son of Man certainly seems to have been the foremost title for Jesus, who used the title far more than all the other ones combined. Although the title of the Son of Man points to the divine heavenly figure of Daniel 7:13, it did not necessarily *only* stress his divinity. To Jesus the title may have meant "both the humility of Christ in assuming mortal flesh," as well as "the glory of Christ as the divine Lord of history."[43] The title "elegantly comprises within itself what for Christians is the central mystery of the incarnation."[44] Yet it

---

[39] God perhaps could have given the authority to forgive sins or to judge humanity to a merely human Messiah, but the evidence nevertheless cumulatively indicates that Jesus was probably not only claiming exclusive divine rights, but that he was also claiming to be God.

[40] Boyarin, *The Jewish Gospels*, xvii (in foreword by Jack Miles); Harry L. Chronis, "To Reveal and to Conceal: A Literary-Critical Perspective on 'the Son of Man' in Mark," *New Testament Studies* 51, no. 4 (October 1, 2005): 477, last accessed November 3, 2013, ATLA Religion Database with ATLASerials, EBSCOhost; Frédéric Lenoir, *Comment Jésus Est Devenu Dieu* (Paris, France: Librairie Arthème Fayard, 2010), 67.

[41] Cf. Boyarin, *The Jewish Gospels*, xvii (in foreword by Jack Miles).

[42] Mark 10:31.

[43] David Bentley Hart, *The Story of Christianity* (New York: Metro Books, 2007), 14.

[44] Ibid.

seems that the title could be applied to him at any time, regardless of whether the Son of Man was Incarnate in human form or not.[45]

If the title had such a significant meaning, why did Jesus not explain it to his disciples at any point in the Gospels? It may be because it was simply not necessary in order for his disciples to know the interpretation of the title.[46] In the pericope of Peter's confession in Matthew 16:13-20, Peter is told that he only came to identify Jesus as the Messiah because it was a revealed to him by God; Peter did not need to interpret the title in order to find out.[47] Furthermore, according to Dalman, Jesus may have wished to present a problem to the crowds (and subsequent readers of the Gospels) which would lead them to deliberate over the identity of Jesus. [48] The reflection over the meaning of "Son of Man" would in turn, for those willing to seek, lead to them finding "fully revealed the mystery of the personality of Jesus."[49] The title may have thus been a parable of sorts for Jesus.[50]

---

[45] Boyarin, *The Jewish Gospels*, 37-38.
[46] Delbert Burkett, *The Son of Man Debate: A History and Evaluation*, (Cambridge, UK: Cambridge University Press, 1999), 69.
[47] Burkett, *The Son of Man Debate*, 69.
[48] Gustaf Dalman, *Words of Jesus Considered in the Light of Post-Biblical Jewish Writings and the Aramaic Language* (Edinburgh, Scotland: Morrison and Gibb Limited, 1902), 259, Google books.
[49] Ibid.
[50] Edward A. McDowell, *Son of Man and Suffering Servant: A Historical and Exegetical Study of Synoptic Narratives Revealing the Consciousness of Jesus Concerning His Person and Mission* (Tennessee: Broadman Press, 1946 3rd printing), 106.

God revealed himself in human form, yet was simultaneously concealed by it.[51] Jesus, whose Hebrew name *Yeshua* means "(the) LORD (is) salvation," was revealed by his name, but he was also disguised by the fact that this name was commonplace in Jesus' time.[52] In the same way, Jesus may have revealed his divine identity in the title of the Son of Man, a title which was also concealed by the fact that it merely meant "the human being" in idiomatic Aramaic.

The concept of a divine Father and a divine Son was not a Christian invention either, having its roots in Daniel (though not exclusively).[53] On the basis of Daniel, the Qumranic texts and the Jewish apocalyptic texts describe Messianic figures who are distinct from God, yet are themselves divine or quasi-divine.[54] The Messianic figure in *4Q246* is even explicitly called "Son of God," and the one from *4 Ezra*, in 7:29, is called "my son."[55]

---

[51] John Parsons, "The Word Made Flesh," *Hebrew for Christians*, last accessed April 23, 2019, http://www.hebrew4christians.com/About_HFC/Site_News/Archive-2013/December/december.html.

[52] Bowman and Komoszewski, *Putting Jesus in His Place*, 2,329 of 4,522; David Flusser, *Jesus* (Jerusalem: The Hebrew University Press, 2001), 302 of 8469, Kindle edition; Erik Larson (class notes); John Parsons, "Is 'Jesus Christ' a Good Jewish Name?" *Hebrew for Christians*, last accessed April 23, 2019, http://www.hebrew4christians.com/Articles/Is_Christ_Jewish_/is_christ_jewish_.html.

[53] Boyarin, *The Jewish Gospels*, 44-47.

[54] Ibid., 71.

[55] Michael E. Stone and Matthias Henze, trans., *4 Ezra and 2 Baruch: Translations, Introductions, and Notes* (Minneapolis, Minnesota: Fortress Press, 2013), 757 of 2,532, Kindle edition; Collins and Collins, *King and Messiah as Son of God*, 66-67, 96.

The prophet Daniel may have been presaging the divine figure's incarnation in human form in Daniel 7:13, for the figure *looks* "like a son of man" and yet is simultaneously divine.[56] The angelic interpretation is not to be excluded,[57] but, being divine, the Danielic "son of man" could not be any angel, but would have to be the unique Angel of the LORD, the King of the angels, who appeared to Moses in the burning bush (Exodus 3:2) and explicitly said, "I am the God of your father, the God of Abraham, the God of Isaac, and the God of Jacob."[58] Angels—including the Angel of the LORD—often appeared to people in human form, but the expression "son of man" may have in addition indicated the unique manner of his manifestation in the world.[59] In Daniel, the angel in 8:15 had "the appearance of a man," and the angel in 10:5 was "a man," but in only the divine figure in 7:13 looked "like a son of man." Angelophanies are sudden

---

[56] Cyril of Alexandria, *Commentary on John: Volume 1*, trans. David R. Maxwell (Illinois: Inter-Varsity Press, 2013), 100; related argument in Dalman, *Words of Jesus*, 242. The divine "son of man" may also be the same figure described by Nebuchadnezzar in Daniel 3:25 as looking "like a son of the gods" ("gods" because Nebuchadnezzar may have believed in other gods besides the God of Daniel and his friends) (See Joseph S. Exell and Henry Donald Maurice Spence-Jones, *The Complete Pulpit Commentary. Volume 5. Isaiah to Daniel. A Exposition, Homiletics, and Homilies Commentary on the Bible* (Harrington, Delaware: Delmarva Publication, 2013), 135,463 of 149,269.

[57] Paul L. Owen, "Problems with Casey's 'Solution'," in *'Who is This Son of Man?': The Latest Scholarship on a Puzzling Expression of the Historical Jesus*, ed. Larry W. Hurtado and Paul L. Owen et al. (New York: Bloomsbury T & T Clark, 2011), 34.

[58] Exodus 3:6.

[59] Robert D. Rowe, "Is Daniel's 'Son of Man' Messianic?" In *Christ the Lord: Studies in Christology presented to Donald Guthrie*, ed. Harold H. Rowdon (Leicester, UK: Inter-Varsity Press, 1982), 91.

and brief in the *Tanakh*, but the Son of Man was born and grew up as a human being. Therefore the Danielic "son of man" would be unique not only in being the Angel of the LORD, but also because he appeared in the world not by suddenly appearing as a man (as angels usually do in the Bible), but by being born of Mary (with "man" in "son of man" being interpreted as a human being),[60] and growing up and living among people for more than thirty years.

B. Conclusion
1. Summary

Chapter 1 provided a short overview of the many interpretations that have been provided throughout the centuries, and pointed out that the debate regarding the Son of Man problem today seems to center around two main interpretations: (1) that the expression was a non-titular idiom and (2) that it was a title derived from Daniel 7:13.

In the second chapter, the various uses of the Aramaic expression בר אנשא (*bar enasha*) were examined. In all the extant Aramaic texts from any time pre-dating Jesus until the time the Talmuds were compiled, "son of man" (whether indefinite or definite) is used either in statements with a generic sense or indefinite sense (although the statements sometimes only refer to one individual). The only occasion pre-dating Jesus (in an extant text in Aramaic) in which "son

---

[60] Tertullian, in "The Five Books Against Marcion," Book IV, Chapter X, Dr. Holmes, trans., in *Ante-Nicene Fathers Volume 3*, by Philip Schaff, ed. Allan Menzies (Michigan: Wm. B Eerdmans Publishing Co., originally published in 1885), 20,364 of 45,166, Kindle edition. Regarding Jesus' use of the title of Son of Man, Burkett states that "most patristic authors preferred the interpretation 'son of Mary,' recognizing that *anthropos* ('human') can refer to woman as well as man" (Burkett, *The Son of Man Debate*, 8).

of man" is referring to a specific individual is in Daniel 7:13, where "one like a son of man" is referring to the Messiah that the prophet Daniel saw in his vision. The chapter also showed how not only the title of Son of Man, but also the allusions to Daniel were distinctive of Jesus as well. As Jesus used the definite article consistently, it was most probably anaphoric, referring each time to the same indefinite "son of man" from Daniel 7:13, the only instance in which "son of man" occurs in Aramaic in the *Tanakh*.

In the exegesis of the Son of Man sayings in Mark, the third chapter showed how Son of Man was a Messianic title, and that Daniel not only was a basis for the title, but that Daniel's thematic and prophetic content was a basis for the content of the Son of Man sayings. Jesus was not using a nontitular idiom; the fact that he was using an expression in Aramaic that was even rare in its indefinite form before his coming already suggested that he was using the expression as more than an idiom. As Jesus was referring to the Messianic figure in Daniel 7:13 each time he uttered the expression, he was indirectly signaling his position as ruler of God's eternal kingdom, which by definition would make the expression a title. Jesus used the title "in exclusively christologically weighted sayings alone,"[61] thereby making the title a Messianic one. When one examines the sayings even further, one realizes that Jesus was using the title not only as a Messianic title, but also as a claim to divinity.

Furthermore, Jesus could not have been referring to another Messianic figure who would come in the future because (1) even if one removes the sayings from their

---

[61] Mogens Müller, *The Expression 'Son of Man' and the Development of Christology: A History of Interpretation* (Sheffield, UK: Equinox, 2012 paperback edition; "First published in hardback in 2008"), 419.

particular narrative contexts, there is nevertheless no evidence anywhere in the New Testament to suggest that someone other than Jesus was expected to come as the Son of Man in the future; (2) most Son of Man sayings unambiguously refer to Jesus; (3) self-reference in the third person was not that infrequent; and (4) the future Son of Man sayings are consistent with those relating to the Son of Man's *present* activity (e.g., Mark 2:10 and 2:28), forming a coherent whole on the basis of Daniel.[62]

2. Implications

The use of the Son of Man title may have also been used by Jesus to preserve his unique Messianic-divine consciousness by distinguishing himself from others,[63] for many have claimed to be the Messiah (or even God) throughout the centuries, but not the Son of Man. In the more than 2,500 years since Daniel had his vision regarding the "son of man," Jesus is the only known person in history to have actually claimed to be the divine "son of man" prophesized in Daniel 7:13.[64] Jesus' claim to divinity is not surprising when one takes into consideration the impact he has had in history, with even the calendar we use being defined by his coming.[65] Jesus would thus not have been

---

[62] Witherington, *The Christology of Jesus*, 247.
[63] McDowell, *Son of Man and Suffering Servant*, 106-107. In the Olivet Discourse, Jesus showed that he was aware that there would be other Messianic claimants when he told his disciples (in Matthew 24:5), "For many will come in my name, saying, 'I am the Christ,' and they will lead many astray."
[64] John J. Collins, *The Scepter and the Star: Messianism in the Light of the Dead Sea Scrolls* (Michigan and Cambridge, UK: Wm. B. Eerdmans Publishing Co., 2010), 237.
[65] Ibid., 233.

divinized by the early church, but the claim to divinity would have originated in the Son of Man himself.[66]

Christian philosopher and theologian William Lane Craig draws out the implications of Jesus' claim to divinity (according to traditional apologetics):

> Jesus claimed to be God, and his claims were either true or false. If they were false, then either he was intentionally lying or else he was deluded. But neither of these alternatives is plausible.[67] Therefore, his claims cannot be false; he must be who he claimed to be, God incarnate, and we must decide whether we shall give our lives to him or not.[68]

All the evidence presented cumulatively indicates that Jesus did indeed claim to be God by the use of the Son of Man title. As a result, after ruling out the two implausible alternatives, one is left with only one choice: that Jesus was (and is) God, as he claimed to be. It would then be up to each individual to decide whether to reject or accept Jesus as their God.[69]

---

[66] Boyarin, *The Jewish Gospels*, 7.
[67] Craig states that the "balance and soundness of Jesus' whole life and teachings make it evident that he was no lunatic" (*Reasonable Faith*, 327). Also, the fact that Jesus persevered with his message in the face of persecution and even death makes it evident that he was sincere.
[68] Craig, *Reasonable Faith*, 299.
[69] Cf. Craig, *Reasonable Faith*, 327.

BIBLIOGRAPHY

Accordance Bible Software. Version 10.

Accordance XII. Version 12.3.4 Lite. April 2019. Copyright © 2019. OakTree Software, Inc. www.accordancebible.com. *Accordance* 10 was used for data and the graphs in this book, and *Accordance XII* was used to verify data and graphs. To the best of my knowledge, only one small change was made: because the ESV was updated in 2016, there is now one additional instance of "lord" in the ESV of the *Tanakh* (see footnote "30" on page 62). *Blue Letter Bible* was also used to verify data ("Changes in the ESV 2016 Version." Last accessed May 16, 2019. https://www.blueletterbible.org/help/esv2016.cfm).

Adams, Edward. "The Coming of the Son of Man in Mark's Gospel." *Tyndale Bulletin* 56, no. 2 (January 1, 2005): 39-61. ATLA Religion Database with ATLASerials, EBSCOhost (last accessed January 10, 2014).

Allison, Jr., Dale C. *The Historical Christ and the Theological Jesus*. Michigan and Cambridge, UK: Wm. B. Eerdmans Publishing Company, 2009. Kindle edition.

Armstrong, Karen. *A History of God*. New York: Ballantine Books, 1993.

Barnes, Albert. "Barnes' Notes on the Bible." *Bible Hub*. http://biblehub.com/commentaries/matthew/26-24.htm (last accessed April 22, 2019), 1834.

Barnes, Albert. "Commentary on Matthew 26:4." "Barnes' Notes on the New Testament." *StudyLight.org*. https://www.studylight.org/commentaries/bnb/matthew-26.html, (last accessed April 22, 2019), 1870.

Barrett, C. K. "The Background of Mark 10:45." In *New Testament Essays: Studies in Memory of T. W. Manson*

1893-1958, edited by A. J. B. Higgins, 1-18. Manchester, UK: The University Press, 1959.

Bauckham, Richard. "The Son of Man: 'A Man in my Position' or 'Someone.'" *Journal for the Study of the New Testament* no. 23 (February 1, 1985): 23-33. ATLA Religion Database with ATLASerials, EBSCOhost (last accessed January 10, 2014).

Blomberg, Craig L. *Jesus and the Gospels: An Introduction and Survey*. 2nd edition. Nashville, Tennessee: B&H Publishing Group, 2009. Kindle edition.

Bock, Darrell L. *Studying the Historical Jesus: A Guide to Sources and Methods*. Michigan: Baker Academic, 2002. Kindle edition.

Boff, Leonardo. *Jesus Christ Liberator: A Critical Christology for Our Time*. Translated by Patrick Hughes. New York: Orbis Books, 1978.

Bowman Jr., Robert M. and J. Ed Komoszewski. *Putting Jesus in His Place: The Case for the Deity of Christ*. Michigan: Kregel Publications, 2007. Kindle edition.

Boyarin, Daniel. *The Jewish Gospels: The Story of the Jewish Christ*. New York: The New Press, 2012 (the paperback edition I used was published in 2013).

Boyarin, Daniel. *The Jewish Gospels: The Story of the Jewish Christ*. New York: The New Press, 2012. Kindle edition.

Branscomb, Bennett Harvie. "Mark 2:5, 'Son Thy Sins Are Forgiven.'" *Journal of Biblical Literature* 53, no. 1 (January 1, 1934): 53-60. ATLA Religion Database with ATLASerials, EBSCOhost (last accessed January 10, 2014).

Bruce, F.F. "The Background to the Son of Man sayings." In *Christ the Lord*, edited by Harold H. Rowdon, 50-70. Leicester, UK: Inter-Varsity Press, 1982.

Bultmann, Rudolf. *The History of the Synoptic Tradition.* Translated by John Marsh. New York and Evanston: Harper & Row, 1968, 2nd ed.

———. *Theology of the New Testament.* Volume I. Translated by Kendrick Grobel. New York: Charles Scribner's Sons, 1951.

Burkett, Delbert. *The Son of Man Debate: A History and Evaluation.* Cambridge, UK: Cambridge University Press, 1999.

Carson, D.A. "Matthew." In *The Expositor's Bible Commentary.* Volume 8, edited by Frank E. Gaebelein. Michigan: Zondervan Pub. House, 1984.

Casey, Maurice. "Aramaic Idiom and the Son of Man Problem: A Response to Owen and Shepherd." *Journal for the Study of the New Testament* 25, no. 1 (September 1, 2002): 3-32. ATLA Religion Database with ATLASerials, EBSCOhost (last accessed January 22, 2014).

———. *The Solution to the 'Son of Man' Problem.* New York: T & T Clark International, 2007. Kindle edition.

Charles, R.H., trans. *The Book of Enoch the Prophet.* Introduction by R. A. Gilbert. New Introduction by Lon Milo DuQuette. California/ Massachusetts: Weiser Books, 2012 ed. Kindle edition.

Charlesworth, James H. in Borg, Marcus J. *Images of Jesus Today.* Edited by James H. Charlesworth and Walter P. Weaver. Valley Forge, Pennsylvania: Trinity Press International, 1994.

Chronis, Harry L. "To Reveal and to Conceal: A Literary-Critical Perspective on 'the Son of Man' in Mark." *New Testament Studies* 51, no. 4 (October 1, 2005): 459-481. ATLA Religion Database with

ATLASerials, EBSCOhost (last accessed November 3, 2013).

Clarke, Adam. "Commentary on the Bible." *Bible Hub*. https://biblehub.com/commentaries/clarke/john/11.htm (last accessed April 22, 2019), 1831.

Clarke, Adam. "Commentary on John 11:9." "The Adam Clarke Commentary." *SudyLight.org*. https://www.studylight.org/commentaries/acc/john-11.html, (last accessed April 22, 2019), 1832.

Colani, Timothée. *Jésus-Christ et les Croyances Messianiques de Son Temps*. Strasbourg, France: Treuttel Et Wurtz, Librairies- Editeurs, 1864.

Collins, Adela Yarbro. "The Origin of the Designation of Jesus as 'Son of Man.'" *Harvard Theological Review* 80, no. 4 (October 1, 1987): 391-407. ATLA Religion Database with ATLASerials, EBSCOhost (last accessed January 22, 2014).

Collins, Adela Yarbro and John J. Collins. *King and Messiah as Son of God: Divine, Human, and Angelic Messianic Figures in Biblical and Related Literature*. Michigan: Wm. B. Eerdmans Publishing Co., 2008.

Collins, John J. *The Scepter and the Star: Messianism in the Light of the Dead Sea Scrolls*. 2nd edition. Michigan and Cambridge, UK: Wm. B. Eerdmans Publishing Co., 2010.

Craig, William Lane. *Reasonable Faith: Christian Truth and Apologetics*. 3rd edition. Illinois: Crossway, 2008.

Crossan, John Dominic. *The Historical Jesus: The Life of a Mediterranean Jewish Peasant*. Harper Collins e-books, 2010. Kindle edition.

Cyril of Alexandria. *Commentary on John: Volume 1.* Translated by David R. Maxwell. Edited by Joel C. Elowsky. Illinois: Inter-Varsity Press, 2013.

Dalman, Gustaf. *Words of Jesus Considered in the Light of Post-Biblical Jewish Writings and the Aramaic Language.* Edinburgh, Scotland: Morrison and Gibb Limited, 1902. Google books.

Drane, John. *Introducing the New Testament: Third Edition.* Minneapolis, Minnesota: Fortress Press, 2011.

Dunn, James D. G. *The Parting of Ways: Between Christianity and Judaism and Their Significance for the Character of Christianity.* London, UK: SCM Press, 1991.

Echegaray, Hugo. *The Practice of Jesus.* Trans. By Matthew O'Connell. New York: Orbis Books, 1984.

Encyclopædia Britannica. "Akiba ben Joseph (Jewish sage and rabbinic founder)." Last accessed April 23, 2019. http://www.britannica.com/EBchecked/topic/11606/Akiba-ben-Joseph.

———. "Hellenistic Age (Ancient Greek History)." Last accessed April 23, 2019. http://www.britannica.com/EBchecked/topic/260307/Hellenistic-Age.

———. "Moses Ibn Ezra." Last accessed April 23, 2019. http://www.britannica.com/EBchecked/topic/280743/Moses-ibn-Ezra.

———. "Targum (Biblical Literature)." Last accessed March 26, 2019. http://www.britannica.com/EBchecked/topic/583515/Targum.

Evans, Craig A. *Ancient Texts for New Testament Studies: A Guide to the Background Literature.* Minneapolis, Minnesota: Baker Academic, 2005.

———. *Fabricating Jesus: How Modern Scholars Distort the Gospels.* Illinois: Inter Varsity Press, 2006. Kindle edition.

———. *Matthew.* New York: Cambridge University Press, 2012.

Exell, Joseph S. and Henry Donald Maurice Spence-Jones. *The Complete Pulpit Commentary. Volume 5. Isaiah to Daniel. A Exposition, Homiletics, and Homilies Commentary on the Bible.* Harrington, Delaware: Delmarva Publication, 2013.

Exell, Joseph S. and Henry Donald Maurice Spence-Jones. *The Complete Pulpit Commentary. Volume 7. Matthew to John. A Exposition, Homiletics, and Homilies Commentary on the Bible.* Harrington, Delaware: Delmarva Publication, 2013.

Fitzmyer, Joseph A. "Another View of the 'Son of Man' Debate." *Journal for the Study of the New Testament* no. 4 (July 1, 1979): 58-68. ATLA Religion Database with ATLASerials, EBSCOhost (last accessed November 10, 2013).

Flusser, David, in collaboration with R. Steven Notley. 3rd edition, corrected and augmented. *Jesus.* Jerusalem: The Hebrew University Press, 2001. Kindle edition.

Frye, Northrop. *The Great Code: The Bible and Literature.* New York/San Diego, California: A Harvest/ HBJ Book, 1983 ed.

Goldwurm, Rabbi Hersh, general editor. *The ArtScroll Series/ Schottenstein Daf Yomi Edition Talmud Bavli/ Tractate Sanhedrin Vol. 1.* New York: Mesorah Publications, Ltd., 2002 edition.

Gutiérrez, Gustavo, et al. "The Option for the Poor Arises from Faith in Christ." *Theological Studies* 70, no. 2 (June 1, 2009): 317-326. ATLA Religion Database with

ATLASerials, EBSCOhost (last accessed January 28, 2014).

Hammond, Edward. *The Books of Enoch*. E-book 2011. Kindle edition.

Hart, David Bentley. *The Story of Christianity*. New York: Metro Books, 2007.

Hartman, Louis F., and Alexander A. Di Lella. *The Book of Daniel*. Translated by Louis F. Hartman. The Anchor Bible. New York: Doubleday, 1978.

Hay, Lewis Scott. "Son of Man in Mark 2:10 and 2:28." *Journal of Biblical Literature* 89, no. 1 (March 1, 1970): 69-75. ATLA Religion Database with ATLASerials, EBSCOhost (last accessed January 10, 2014).

Higgins, A.J.B. *Jesus and the Son of Man*. Pennsylvania: Fortress Press, 1964.

Holladay, William L., ed. *A Concise Hebrew and Aramaic Lexicon of the Old Testament*. Michigan: Wm. B. Eerdmans Publishing Co., 1988.

Hooker, Morna Dorothy. "Is the Son of Man Problem Really Insoluble?" In *Text and Interpretation: Studies in the New Testament Presented to Matthew Black*, edited by Ernest Best and R.McL. Wilson, 155-168. Cambridge, UK: Cambridge University Press, 1979.

Horbury, William. *Jewish Messianism and the Cult of Christ*. London, UK: SCM Press Ltd, 1998.

Hurtado, Larry W. and Paul L. Owen et al. *'Who is This Son of Man?': The Latest Scholarship on a Puzzling Expression of the Historical Jesus*. Edited by Larry W. Hurtado and Paul L. Owen. New York: Bloomsbury T & T Clark, 2011.

Jamieson, Robert, A.R. Fausset, and David Brown. "A Commentary, Critical, Practical, and Explanatory on the Old and New Testaments." *Bible Hub.* http://biblehub.com/commentaries/mark/2-7.htm (last accessed April 26, 2019). http://biblehub.com/commentaries/mark/9-31.htm (last accessed April 26, 2019), 1882.

Jamieson, Robert, A.R. Fausset, and David Brown. "Commentary Critical and Explanatory on the Whole Bible." *Christian Classics Ethereal Library.* http://www.ccel.org/ccel/jamieson/jfb.txt (last accessed April 26, 2019), 1871.

Jeremias, Joachim. *New Testament Theology.* New York: Charles Scribner's Sons, 1971.

Johansson, Daniel. "'Who Can Forgive Sins but God Alone?' Human and Angelic Agents, and Divine Forgiveness in Early Judaism." *Journal for the Study of the New Testament* 33, no. 4 (June 1, 2011): 351-374. ATLA Religion Database with ATLASerials, EBSCOhost (last accessed January 18, 2014).

Johnson, Barton W. "The People's New Testament." *Bible Hub.* https://biblehub.com/commentaries/pnt/mark/2.htm (last accessed April 26, 2019), 1891.

Johnson, S.E. "Son of Man." In *Interpreter's Dictionary of the Bible.* Volume 4. New York/ Tennessee: Abingdon Press, 1962.

Kee, Howard Clarke. "Christology in Mark's Gospel." *Judaisms and Their Messiahs at the Turn of the Christian Era.* Edited by Jacob Neusner, William Scoot Green, and Ernest S. Frerichs. New York: Cambridge University Press, 1987.

Kittel, Bonnie Pedrotti ; Victoria Hoffer, and Rebecca Abts Wright. *Biblical Hebrew Text and Workbook: Second Edition.* Fully revised by Victoria Hoffer. Connecticut: Yale University Press, 2005.

Lauterbach, Jacob Z. *Mekilta de-Rabbi Ishmael.* Volume Three. Pennsylvania: The Jewish Publication Society of America, 1935.

Lenoir, Frédéric. *Comment Jésus Est Devenu Dieu.* Paris, France: Librairie Arthème Fayard, 2010.

Lindars, Barnabas. *Jesus Son of Man: A Fresh Examination of the Son of Man sayings in the Gospels in the Light of Recent Research.* Michigan: Wm. B. Eerdmans, 1983.

———. "Re-Enter the Apocalyptic Son of Man." *New Testament Studies* 21, no. 1 (October, 1975): 52-72.

Long, Didier. *Jésus de Nazareth, Juif de Galilée.* Paris, France: Presses de la Renaissance, 2011.

———. *L'Invention du Christianisme: Et Jésus Devint Dieu.* Paris, France: Presses de la Renaissance, 2012.

Longenecker, Richard N. "'Son of Man' as a Self-Designation of Jesus." *Journal of The Evangelical Theological Society* 12, no. 3 (June 1, 1969): 151-158. ATLA Religion Database with ATLASerials, EBSCOhost (last accessed January 22, 2014).

MacArthur, John. *Twelve Ordinary Men: How the Master Shaped His Disciples for Greatness and What He Wants to Do with You.* Nashville, Tennessee: Thomas Nelson, 2002. Kindle edition.

Macho, Alejandro Díez. "La Cristología del Hijo del Hombre y el Uso de la Tercera Persona en Vez de la Primera." *Scripta Theologica* 14, no. 1 (January 1, 1982): 189-201. ATLA Religion Database with ATLASerials, EBSCOhost (last accessed January 22, 2014).

Marcus, Joel. "Mark 14:61 : 'Are you the Messiah-Son-of-God?'" *Novum Testamentum* 31, no. 2 (April 1, 1989): 125-141. ATLA Religion Database with ATLASerials, EBSCOhost (last accessed September 28, 2013).

Martin, Martina E. "It's My Prerogative: Jesus' Authority to Grant Forgiveness and Healing on Earth." *Journal Of Religious Thought* 59, (January 1, 2007): 67-74. ATLA Religion Database with ATLASerials, EBSCOhost (last accessed January 18, 2014).

McDowell, Edward A. *Son of Man and Suffering Servant: A Historical and Exegetical Study of Synoptic Narratives Revealing the Consciousness of Jesus Concerning His Person and Mission.* Tennessee: Broadman Press, 1946 (3rd printing).

Milavec, Aaron. *The Didache: Text, Translation, Analysis, and Commentary.* Translated by Aaron Milavec. Minnesota: Liturgical Press, 2003.

Morgenstern, Julian. "'Son of Man' of Daniel 7:13f: A New Interpretation." *Journal of Biblical Literature* 80, no. 1 (March 1, 1961): 65-77. ATLA Religion Database with ATLASerials, EBSCOhost (last accessed January 22, 2014).

Moule, C.F.D. *The Origin of Christology.* Cambridge, UK: Cambridge University Press, 1977.

Müller, Metzger, Bruce Manning, and Michael David Coogan. *The Oxford Companion to the Bible.* New York: Oxford University Press, 1993.

Müller, Mogens. *The Expression 'Son of Man' and the Development of Christology: A History of Interpretation.* Sheffield, UK: Equinox, 2012 paperback edition; "First published in hardback in 2008."

Müller, Peter. "Zwischen dem Gekommenen und dem Kommenden: Intertextuelle Aspekte der Menschensohnaussagen im Markusevangelium." In *Gottessohn und Menschesohn: Exegetische Studien zu Zwei Paradigmen Biblischer Intertextualität*, edited Dieter Sänger. *Biblisch-Theologische Studien 67*, edited by Jörg Frey, Ferdinand Hahn, Bernd Janowski, Werner H. Schmidt, and Wolfgang Schrage. Neukirchen-Vluyn, Germany: Neukirchener, 2004, 130-157.

Neusner, Jacob. *The Talmud of the Land of Israel: An Academic Commentary to the Second, Third, and Fourth Divisions: VIII. Yerushalmi Tractate Taanit*. Georgia, USA: Scholars Press, 1998.

NIV New Testament (Red Letter Edition). Michigan: Zondervan, 2011. Kindle edition.

NLT Parallel Study Bible. Senior Editor Comfort, Philip W. Carol Stream, Illinois: Tyndale House Publishers, Inc., 2011.

Nolan, Albert. *Jesus Before Christianity*. New York: Orbis Books, 1992.

Novo, Alfonso. "El Hijo del Hombre en los Evangelios Sinópticos." *Estudios Eclesiásticos* 75, no. 292 (January 1, 2000): 23-78. ATLA Religion Database with ATLASerials, EBSCOhost (last accessed January 22, 2014).

O'Collins, Gerald, S.J. *What Are They Saying About Jesus?* New York: Paulist Press, 1977.

Owen, Paul, and David Shepherd. "Speaking Up for Qumran, Dalman and the Son of Man: Was Bar Enasha a Common Term for 'Man' in the Time of Jesus?" *Journal for the Study of the New Testament* no. 81 (March 1, 2001): 81-122. ATLA Religion Database with ATLASerials, EBSCOhost (last accessed January 18, 2014).

Parsons, John. "Is 'Jesus Christ' a Good Jewish Name?" *Hebrew for Christians.* http://www.hebrew4christians.com/Articles/Is_Christ_Jewish_/is_christ_jewish_.html (last accessed April 23, 2019).

———. "The Word Made Flesh..." *Hebrew for Christians.* http://www.hebrew4christians.com/About_HFC/Site_News/Archive-2013/December/december.html (last accessed April 23, 2019).

———. "Yeshua is LORD." *Hebrew for Christians.* www.hebrew4christians.com/Names_of_G-d/Yeshua_is_Adonai/yeshua_is_adonai.html (last accessed April 23, 2019).

Perrin, Norman. "Son of Man in Ancient Judaism and Primitive Christianity: A Suggestion." *Biblical Research* 11, (January 1, 1966): 17-28. ATLA Religion Database with ATLASerials, EBSCOhost (last accessed March 14, 2019).

———. "Son of Man in the Synoptic tradition." *Biblical Research* 13, (January 1, 1968): 3-25. ATLA Religion Database with ATLASerials, EBSCOhost (last accessed October 20, 2013).

———. *The Promise of Bultmann.* Pennsylvania: Fortress Press, 1969.

Robinson, James M., Paul Hoffmann, and John S. Kloppenborg, ed. Milton C. Moreland, managing ed. *The Sayings: Gospel Q in Greek and English: With Parallels from the Gospels of Mark and Thomas.* Minneapolis, Minnesota: Fortress Press, 2002.

Rowe, Robert D. "Is Daniel's 'Son of Man' Messianic?" In *Christ the Lord: Studies in Christology presented to Donald Guthrie*, edited by Harold H. Rowdon. Leicester, UK: Inter-Varsity Press, 1982, 71-96.

Sanders, E.P. *Judaism: Practice and Belief 63 BCE-66 CE*. Pennsylvania: Trinity Press International, 1992.

Schaberg, Jane. "Daniel 7, 12 and the New Testament Passion-Resurrection Predictions." *New Testament Studies* 31, no.2 (1985): 208-222.

Schaff, Philip. *Ante-Nicene Fathers Volume 3*. Edited by Allan Menzies. Michigan: Wm. B Eerdmans Publishing Co., originally published in 1885. Kindle edition.

Scheifler, José Ramón. "El Hijo del Hombre en Daniel." *Estudios Eclesiásticos* 34, no. 134-135 (July 1, 1960): 789-804. ATLA Religion Database with ATLASerials, EBSCOhost (last accessed January 22, 2014).

Schillebeeckx, Edward. *Jesus: An Experiment in Christology*. New York: The Seabury Press, 1979.

Schwartz, Regina M. "Joseph's Bones and the Resurrection of the Text: Remembering in the Bible." *PMLA* 103, no. 2 (March, 1988): 114-124. Published by Modern Language Association. JSTOR. https://www.jstor.org/stable/462428 (last accessed April 7, 2019).

———. *The Curse of Cain: The Violent Legacy of Monotheism*. Chicago: The University of Chicago Press, 1997.

Spence, H.D.M. "Pulpit Commentary." *Bible Hub*. http://biblehub.com/commentaries/daniel/3-25.htm; http://biblehub.com/commentaries/daniel/7-25.htm;

http://biblehub.com/commentaries/matthew/9-6.htm; http://biblehub.com/commentaries/mark/2-28.htm (last accessed April 27, 2019).

Stone, Michael E. "The Messiah in 4 Ezra." *Judaisms and Their Messiahs at the Turn of the Christian Era.* Edited by Jacob Neusner, William Scoot Green, and Ernest S. Frerichs. New York: Cambridge University Press, 1987.

Stone, Michael E. and Matthias Henze. *4 Ezra and 2 Baruch: Translations, Introductions, and Notes.* Translated by Michael E. Stone and Matthias Henze. Minneapolis, Minnesota: Fortress Press, 2013. Kindle edition.

Taylor, Vincent. *The Gospel According to St. Mark.* London, UK: Macmillan & Co. Ltd., 1959.

The Holy Bible, English Standard Version. ESV Text Edition: 2011. Illinois: Crossway, 2011.

The New Oxford American Dictionary. Second Edition. New York: Oxford University Press, Inc e-book, 2010. Kindle edition.

Vermes, Geza. *Jesus the Jew.* Pennsylvania: Fortress Press, 1973.

———. *The Changing Faces of Jesus.* New York: Penguin Books, 2000.

———, trans. *The Complete Dead Sea Scrolls in English.* London, UK/ New York: Penguin Books, 2011, 5th edition. Kindle edition.

———. "The 'Son of Man' Debate." *Journal for the Study of the New Testament* no. 1 (October 1, 1978): 19-32. ATLA Religion Database with ATLASerials, EBSCOhost (last accessed January 8, 2014).

Wadud, Amina. *Qur'an and Woman: Rereading the Sacred Text from a Woman's Perspective.* New York: Oxford

University Press, 1999. ACLS Humanities E-book. http://hdl.handle.net/2027/heb.04755 (e-book last accessed March 3, 2019).

Wadud-Muhsin, Amina. *Qur'an and Woman*. Kuala Lumpur: Penerbit Fajar Bakti Sdn. Bhd., 1993, 2nd edition.

Walker, Norman. "After Three Days." *Novum Testamentum* 4, no. 4 (December 1, 1960): 261-262. ATLA Religion Database with ATLASerials, EBSCOhost (last accessed February 27, 2014).

Wigram, George V. "Englishman's Concordance." *Bible Hub*. http://biblehub.com/hebrew/yahweh_3068.htm (last accessed April 16, 2019).

Witherington, III, Ben. *The Christology of Jesus*. Minneapolis, Minnesota: Fortress Press, 1990.

———. *The Gospel of Mark: A Socio-Rhetorical Commentary*. Michigan and Cambridge, UK: William B. Eerdmans Publishing Company, 2001. Kindle edition.

Wright, N.T. *Jesus and the Victory of God: Christian Origins and the Question of God, Volume 2*. London, UK: Fortress Press, 1996. Kindle edition.

www.ingramcontent.com/pod-product-compliance
Lightning Source LLC
Chambersburg PA
CBHW041431300426
44116CB00001B/4